Real Estate Reference Guide For Judges and Law Clerks

Office of the Ramsey County Examiner of Titles
Wayne D. Anderson, Examiner
Nathan A. Bissonette, Deputy

Version 7.1   July 1, 2023

Introduction

Judges come from varied backgrounds and may rotate through subject-matter-specific courts but sooner or later, all judges will be assigned a case involving real estate issues. For judges who last encountered those topics as a 1L, there can be a steep learning curve. In cases with *pro se* defendants or ill-prepared attorneys, the Court cannot depend on the parties to illuminate the issues. When the blind lead the blind, justice is not the most likely destination.

Real estate law is broad enough and complex enough to warrant its own specialist certification by the Minnesota State Bar Association. This guide is intended neither to make you a real estate specialist nor to substitute for the pleadings and briefs submitted in your case. This guide is intended to give you a jump-start on legal research, to check the assertions made in the pleadings and briefs, and to raise issues the parties may have failed to consider.

The first part of each topic section is an overview, suitable to print and carry to the bench for quick reference during oral argument. It's a red-flag list, intended to raise points to question during argument or to request later briefing, such as "Necessary Parties."
The latter part of each topic section provides citations to landmark cases. This part is intended for use when reading the briefs and writing the decision. Of course, you will do your own legal research and reach your own conclusions. We're simply providing a common starting point. Updates are added at the end of the relevant section, to make them easier to find.

This guide grew out of a series of conversations with judges of District Court, who provided valuable guidance along the way. This guide was researched and written by Nathan Bissonette, Deputy Examiner for Ramsey County, then circulated in draft form for peer review.

Real Estate Reference Guide for Judges

More than a dozen practicing real estate lawyers suggested changes and improvements, including major contributions to these sections by:

>Contracts for Deed and Purchase Agreements: Larry Wertheim, Kennedy and Graven
>Inverse Condemnation: David B. Gates, Deputy Examiner of Titles, Hennepin County
>Streets: Kim Brzezinski, St. Louis County Examiner of Titles; Scott Lucas, Olson, Lucas, Redford & Wahlberg, P.A

A word about citations:

In the days when lawyers looked up cases in books, it was proper to include both the Minnesota and Northwest numbers. Electronic legal research makes one citation sufficient. Unpublished opinions are not precedential but, where one offers a particularly good explanation of the law, the citation is given without attaching a copy of the opinion because you'll be doing more research anyway.

Remember to search:

Some cases affect several topics but may not appear in all sections. For example, the rights of a landowner whose lands abut a lakeside street may found in Streets, Riparian Rights, or both. We recommend you use the "find" function to search for topics, in addition to the Table of Contents.

Copyright:

Ramsey County has dedicated this work to the public domain. It is not protected by copyright.

Contents

"Abstract" versus "Torrens"	5
Adverse Possession	10
Attorney Lien	16
Boundary Determination	18
Condemnation – Eminent Domain	22
Contract for Deed and Purchase Agreement Cancellation Primer	28
Contract for Deed – deed in fulfillment not delivered	31
Contract for Deed – enjoin statutory cancellation	34
Constitutional Lien	40
Easements	42
Equitable subrogation	52
Foreclosure by Action (of a mortgage)	55
Foreclosure by Advertisement (of a mortgage)	59
Inverse Condemnation	64
Jurisdiction and Venue	69
Legal Descriptions	71
Life estate	75
Marital Lien	77
Marital Rights	80
Marketable Title Act (40-year law)	83
Mechanic's Lien	86
Name	97
Option, Right of First Refusal, Right of First Offer	99
Partition	105
Practical Location	108
Priority – Recording Act	116

Real Estate Reference Guide for Judges

Purchase Agreement – Enjoin Cancellation or Recover Earnest Money (Residential Only) 118

Purchase Agreement - Specific Performance to Compel Closing.122

Quiet Title (Action to Determine Adverse Claims)........................125

Redemption..129

Reformation of a Document 139

Restrictive Covenants (30-year law) 143

Riparian Rights 146

Slander of Title 154

Sovereign Citizen Claims 157

Specific Performance to compel sale closing 159

Statute of Frauds...163

Streets and Access – Overview 166

Streets and Access – Abandonment..170

Streets and Access - Cartway 173

Streets and Access – Implied Easements and Easements by Necessity..182

Streets and Access – Prescriptive Easements 188

Streets and Access – Statutory User and Common Law Dedication 193

Streets and Access – Vacation...198

Tenancy 207

Transfer on Death Deed..214

Trespass 217

Version 7.1   July 1, 2023

"Abstract" versus "Torrens"

First Question in Every Real Estate Case: Is the Land Abstract or Torrens?

Minnesota has two systems of land records operating simultaneously and in parallel: 1) the "abstract" system operated by the County Recorder; 2) and the registered property or "Torrens" system operated by the Registrar of Titles (named after its inventor, Robert Torrens). The two systems have different enabling legislation, different purposes and different rules.
Your default presumption is that the land in your case is abstract. Red Flag Words that this is a Torrens case: Registrar of Titles, Certificate of Title, Minn. Stat. Chapter 508. You should see Torrens cases only after the Examiner of Titles has reviewed the court file and written a Report of Examiner.

Broadly:

> If the requested relief **primarily** involves altering a Certificate of Title, it **must be** handled as a Torrens case including a Report of Examiner. Examples include:
>
>> Issue a new Certificate of Title following foreclosure by advertisement
>> Change the legal description or owner's name on a Certificate of Title
>> Alter or remove a memorial of an easement or lien from a Certificate of Title

This requirement is jurisdictional and failure to comply is fatal.
Phillips v. Dolphin, 776 N.W.2d 755 (Minn. App. 2009);
Rule 215 Minn. Gen. R. Prac.

If you get a case involving Torrens land but there is no Report of Examiner in the Court file, please call the Examiner of Titles to ask why not.

Real Estate Reference Guide for Judges

If there is a Report of Examiner, it should tell you what law controls, what facts will be relevant, what evidence you need to establish those facts, the required Defendants, and what Order is recommended.

If the requested relief **incidentally** involves lands shown on a Certificate of Title, that case should be handled as if the lands were abstract. The Examiner of Titles is not ordinarily involved in these actions. Examples include:

>Award property in a divorce
>Restore possession in an eviction
>Probate of an Estate
>Reduced mortgage redemption period following foreclosure

Certain cases involving title to Torrens land are not brought as a Proceeding Subsequent, i.e. where there is a separate statutory procedure that overrides the Torrens act. Those cases are:

>Attorney Lien Foreclosure
>Condemnation and Inverse Condemnation
>Mechanic's Lien Foreclosure
>Mortgage Foreclosure by Action
>Partition
>Street Vacation by Judicial Action

Citations:

Britney v. Swan Lake Cabin Corp., 795 N.W.2d 867, 870 (Minn. App. 2011) (citing *In re Geis,* 576 N.W.2d 747, 749-50 (Minn. App. 1998), review denied (Minn. May 28, 1998), for the proposition that matters related to Torrens properties are governed by the Torrens Act);

When an applicant fails to follow the procedural requirements of the Torrens Act, the district court must dismiss the action. See *Britney,* 795 N.W.2d at 871.

Phillips v. Dolphin, 776 N.W.2d 755, 758 (Minn. App. 2009) ("When the Torrens Act specifies the procedure necessary to take some action regarding registered land, parties and district courts must follow this procedure.") Review denied (Minn. Mar. 16, 2010); *Park Elm Homeowner's Ass'n v. Mooney*, 398 N.W.2d 643, 646-47 (Minn. App. 1987) (holding that the district court lacked authority to issue an order that adversely affected title to registered lands because the district court did not comply with the Torrens Act).

". . . caselaw firmly establishes that failure to follow Torrens Act procedures precludes consideration of claims to establish the boundaries of registered property. To the extent that the provisions of the Torrens Act conflict with chapter 559, we apply the more particular provisions of the Torrens Act in this proceeding. See Minn. Stat. § 645.26, subd. 1(2012) (setting forth rule of statutory construction that when a special provision in one statute is in irreconcilable conflict with a general provision in another statute, "the special provision shall prevail").

The district court did not err by dismissing Rechtzigel's complaint for failure to comply with the procedural requirements of section 508.671 and Minn. R. Gen. Prac. 211.3. . . .."
> *In the Matter of the Application of Gene Rechtzigel*, unpublished, A14-0449 (Minn. App. 2014)

SEE ALSO:

> *In the Matter of Metro Siding, Inc.*, 624 N.W.2d 303 (Minn. App. 2001)

> *Walther v. Lundberg*, 654 N.W.2d 694 (Minn. App., 2002)

> *In the Matter of Prime Security Bank*, unpublished, A14-0784 (Minn. App. 2015)

Real Estate Reference Guide for Judges

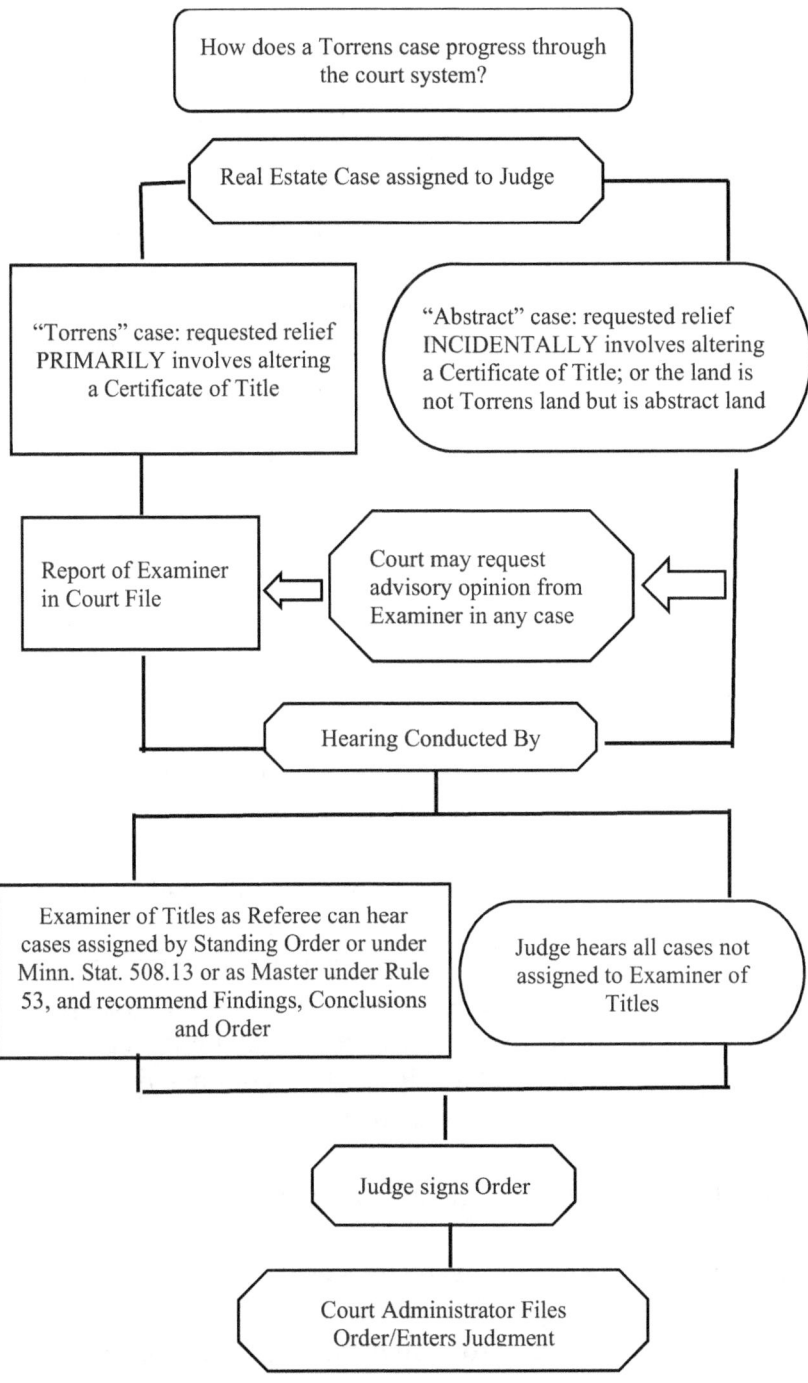

Version 7.1   July 1, 2023

Adverse Possession

Summary	An action to confirm that a person acquired title to land based on possession instead of conveyance
Statute	Usually pled as Declaratory Judgment under Chapter 555, Action to Determine Adverse Claims under Minn. Stat. 559.01, or to Determine Boundary Line under Minn. Stat. 559.23
Limitations	Minn. Stat. 541.02 – cannot bring the claim until 15 years have passed
Necessary Parties	Landowner of record, lien holders, occupants, encroachers, persons known to Plaintiff to have a claim or interest that does not appear of record
Elements	Actual, open, notorious, hostile, exclusive, continuous possession for 15 years
	If the land claimed is an entire parcel that is separately taxed, claimant must have paid the taxes on the entire parcel for some five-consecutive-year portion of the 15-year period of adverse possession. A claim for a portion of a parcel to adjust a boundary line does not require tax payment.
Burden of Proof	Person seeking to gain title
Standard of Proof	Clear and convincing
Defenses	Must prove all elements; failure on any is fatal

Real Estate Reference Guide for Judges

Oddities	Claimant can "tack" a prior owner's time of adverse possession to claimant's time of adverse possession if there is privity between owners
	Not available against land owned by a public entity
	Action to Determine Boundary Lines under Minn. Stat. 559.23 is separate action but may include claim of ownership by Adverse Possession
Special Torrens Note	Adverse Possession is not available against land already registered (Minn. Stat. 508.02), but adverse possession can be used to establish title in the initial registration. Minn. Stat. 508.03, 508.06; *Petition of Building D, Inc.,* 502 N.W.2d 406 (Minn. App. 1993) Exceptions:

      a. Claimant (or claimant's predecessors in interest whose time can be tacked) had an adverse possession claim at the time the property was initially registered; the adverse possession claim was not adjudicated in the initial registration; and the adverse possession claim is not a collateral attack on the initial registration.

      Minneapolis & St. Louis Railway Company v. Ellsworth, 54 N.W.2d 800 (1952); *Petition of McGinnis,* 536 N.W.2d 33 (Minn. App. 1995)

b. The legal descriptions of claimant's land and the claimed land are so ambiguous the court can't tell what was registered to whom.

Petition of Zahradka, 472 N.W.2d 153 (Minn. App. 1991)

Rule 215 Minn. Gen. R. Prac. requires an order in a civil case that affects Torrens land to be approved as to form by Examiner of Titles before presentation to court.

Citations
Actual, open, hostile, exclusive and continuous possession.
Ehle v. Prosser, 197 N.W.2d 458 (Minn. 1972)

For at least 15 years
Minn. Stat. 541.02. *Romans v. Nadler*, 14 N.W.2d 482 (Minn. 1944)

But claimant can "tack" a prior owner's time of adverse possession to claimant's time of adverse possession if there is privity between owners.
Fredericksen v. Henke, 209 N.W. 257 (1926)

The possession must give "unequivocal notice to the true owner that someone is in possession in hostility to his title."
Ganje v. Schuler, 659 N.W.2d 261, 266 (Minn. App. 2003) citing *Skala v. Lindbeck*, 214 N.W. 271, 272 (Minn. 1927)

"Claims relating to boundary lines of lands and claims to lands not assessed for taxation as separate tracts . . . are

clearly exempt from the statutory provisions requiring the payment of taxes."
>*Ehle v. Prosser*, 197 N.W.2d 458, 462 (Minn. 1972)

And if the land being claimed is an entire parcel that is separately taxed (not just a sliver of a parcel to adjust a boundary), claimant must have paid the taxes on the entire parcel for some five-consecutive-year period of the 15-year period of adverse possession.
>Minn. Stat. 541.02. *Grubb v. State*, 433 N.W.2d 915 (Minn. App. 1988)

Must prove all elements; failure on any is fatal.
>*Johnson v. Raddohl*, 32 N.W.2d 860 (Minn. 1948)

Not available against land in use by the public.
>Minn. Stat. 541.01
>*Fischer v. City of Sauk Rapids*, 325 N.W.2d 816, 819 (Minn. 1982)

Burden of Proof is on the person trying to seize title and the Standard of Proof is clear and convincing evidence.
>*Ehle v. Prosser,* 197 N.W.2d. 458 (Minn. 1972)

Order should include:

1) Findings of Fact reciting the evidence for each factor including length of time of adverse possession and dates of payment of taxes, if relevant

2) Conclusion of Law stating evidence was clear and convincing

3) The legal description of all the lands owned by the acquiring party including the newly-acquired

lands, and a legal description of the residue lands still owned by the disseized party

2018 update:

Sporadic and occasional recreational or seasonal use does not demonstrate "actual possession" but other uses may satisfy that element.
> *Aydt v. Hensel*, unpublished, A17-0448 (Minn. App. 2017)

A continuous period of "hostile" possession may be interrupted.
> *Compart v. Wolfstellar*, 906 N.W.2d 598 (Minn. App. 2018)

Co-tenants are presumed to share the land, a permissive use which defeats the "hostile" element of an adverse possession claim. The presumption can be rebutted.
> *Jokela v. Jokela*, unpublished, A11-1247 (Minn. App. 2012)

2020 update:

Disputed tree lines were not sufficient to establish the boundary by practical location and Plaintiff's evidence of occupation was not sufficient to support adverse possession of all the disputed land. Remanded for a survey and legal description of the lands adversely possessed.
> *Batton v. Hawk*, unpublished, A19-0289 (Minn. App. 2019)

Under Minn. Stat. 541.02, a person claiming ownership by adverse possession of "substantially all" of a parcel must have paid the taxes on it for at least five years.
> *St. Paul Park Refining Co., LLC v. Domeier*, A19-0573, Minn. App. 2020). **NOTE:** the Supreme Court

granted review of this decision. The issue on appeal is likely to be what constitutes "substantially all."

2021 update:
Adverse possession requires clear and convincing evidence of "open" possession, proven by aerial photos showing the 'green triangle' stood in sharp contrast to surrounding farmland.

Klug v. Ellenz, unpublished, A20-1479 (Minn. App. 2021)

The requirement to have paid taxes on lands claimed by adverse possession does not apply to boundary disputes but does apply when the lands claimed are less than the full assessed parcel, but how much is enough to trigger the requirement? In *Grubb v. State*, 433 N.W.2d 915 (Minn. App. 1988), the disseizor claimed 80% and was required to pay taxes. In *Compart v. Wolfstellar*, 906 N.W.2d 598, 602 (Minn. App. 2018), review denied (Minn. Apr. 17, 2018), the disseizor claimed 20% and was not required to pay taxes. The legislative intent underlying Section 541.02 is to apply the tax-payment requirement 'actions where the disseizor claims all or substantially all of an assessed tract or parcel. *Grubb*, 433 N.W.2d 915, at 920. In this case, Domeier claimed 5.32% of the East parcel and was not required to have paid taxes on that land; but claimed 52% of the West parcel and, since he had failed to pay taxes on that parcel, his adverse possession claim failed.

St. Paul Park Refining Co. LLC, v. Domeier, 938 N.W.2d 288 (Minn. App. 2020).

Attorney Lien

Summary	Attorney can file a lien on land for unpaid professional services relating to that parcel of land
Statute	Minn. Stat. 481.13, Subd. 2(a)
Limitations	Must record lien within 120 days of last item of claimed service
	Must commence lien foreclosure within one year after filing lien statement (owner may agree in writing to extend to three years)
Necessary Parties	Landowner of record, lien holders, occupants
Elements	Land was involved in or affected by attorney's services
	Lien amount is reasonable value of attorney's services
Burden of Proof	Lien claimant
Standard of Proof	Preponderance
Defenses	Value of work, land not affected by attorney services
Oddities	The lien statute allows a lien on a homestead. Lawyer's Board of Professional Responsibility Opinion No. 14 formerly restricted attorney liens on client homesteads but was repealed in 2003 when the present statute was enacted. The lien is subject to

homestead exemption unless a valid waiver is obtained. Minn. Stat. 510.05

Attorneys also may assert liens on causes of action such as settlement funds or funds in an estate; those are outside the scope of this discussion.

Failure to timely file lien or commence foreclosure is fatal, but a personal judgment on account stated, contract or *quantum meruit* might lie.

Special Torrens Note	If the land is Torrens, the attorney's lien must be timely recorded on the Certificate of Title to be enforceable. A lien recorded in the abstract records is not enforceable against Torrens land.

An attorney's lien foreclosure is really a breach of contract claim, the foreclosure is merely a procedure to collect the resulting judgment; therefore, the primary purpose of the action is not to alter a Certificate of Title, so this is not a "Torrens" case and a Report of Examiner is not needed; but title will not transfer without a Certificate of Examiner approving the Order, issued under Minn. Stat. 508.59.

Citations	*Boline v. Doty,* 345 N.W.2d 285 (Minn. App. 1984); but see *Xiong v. Dubbles* A12-1898 unpublished (Minn. App. 2013) on summary nature of proceeding.

Thomas A. Foster & Associates, Ltd, v. Paulson, 699 N.W.2d 1 (Minn. App. 2005)

Boundary Determination

Summary	Action for judicial determination of boundary line. Usually brought because one party claims title by adverse possession or practical location and wants judicial landmarks placed to avoid future conflict
Statute	Minn. Stat. 508.671, 559.23
Limitations	None
Necessary Parties	Owner of land on which boundary is sought to be located, owners of adjacent lands affected by the determination of the boundary line, holders of encumbrances and encroachments whose interest will be affected by changing the line
Elements	)
Burden of Proof	)
Standard of Proof	) Depends on underlying theory of law
Defenses	)
Oddities	Two-step procedure. Both statutes require Plaintiff to file a Certificate of Survey from a Licensed Land Surveyor in the court file showing the proposed location of the line, then the court holds the trial taking evidence whether the proposed line is the correct line and makes a decision where the boundary line should be located. An Interlocutory Order is entered stating the location of the boundary line, which also directs the surveyor to go back to place Judicial Landmarks to monument the boundary line that the Court has decided on, and also to file a new

Real Estate Reference Guide for Judges

Certificate of Survey in the court file showing the new line and location where Judicial Landmarks were set. After the updated Certificate of Survey is filed in the Court file, a second hearing is held to confirm the location where the Judicial Landmarks were set was correct, after which the Final Order is issued.

Special Torrens Note

Boundaries can be registered during a proceeding for initial registration under Minn. Stat. 508.06 (11) or in a Proceeding Subsequent to Initial Registration brought under Minn. Stat. 508.671.

Rule 215 Minn. Gen. R. Prac. requires an order in a civil case that affects Torrens land to be approved as to form by Examiner of Titles before presentation to court.

Citations

A tribal court does not have authority under Minn. Stat. 508.671 to judicially establish boundary lines in a proceeding subsequent, to property not included in the original registration. *Petition of Geis*, 576 N.W.2d 747 (Minn. App. 1998).

Abstract and Torrens lands:

If the lands on both sides of the boundary to be determined are abstract lands, the boundary is set in a District Court action pursuant to Minn. Stat. 559.23.

If the lands on both sides of the boundary to be determined are Torrens lands, and those boundaries were not set in the original registration proceeding, the boundary is set in a Proceeding Subsequent to Initial Registration pursuant to Minn. Stat. 508.671. That section is the exclusive method for setting boundaries on real property that is already registered.

If the land on one side of the boundary to be determined is abstract and the other side is Torrens, the boundary must be established in a Proceeding Subsequent. Minnesota Statutes section 508.671, subdivision 1 was amended in 2017 to clarify that the court's order from the Pro Sub can cover both Torrens and abstract lands and must be recorded in both recording systems.

> *Britney v. Swan Lake Cabin Corp.*, 795 N.W.2d 867 (Minn. App. 2011)
> *Phillips v. Dolphin*, 776 N.W.2d 755 (Minn. App. 2009)

Other helpful cases:

> *Petition of Ruikkie v. Nall*, 798 N.W.2d 806 (Minn. App. 2011)
> *Theros v. Phillips*, 256 N.W.2d 852 (Minn. 1977)

Real Estate Reference Guide for Judges

2018 update:
Boundary cases are among the hardest to settle because the issues are personal and emotional: it's "my land" and "a matter of principle." See, for example, *In re the Petition of Melvin J. Cummins,* unpublished, A14-0737 (Minn. App. 2015) (litigating a boundary line); appealed again at 906 N.W.2d 280 (Minn. App. 2017) (litigating the time to appeal from the boundary decision); and appealed a third time in an unpublished opinion, A17-1568 (Minn. App. 2018) (reversing the 2011 trial court's determination because evidence a prior owner acquiesced in a fence line was not clear and convincing).

The boundary dispute can generate self-help remedies that escalate into a Harassment Restraining Order.
Olsen v. Greger, unpublished, A17-0245 (Minn. App. 2017)

Nathan Bissonette

Condemnation – Eminent Domain

Summary	Government taking private land for public use. The power of the sovereign to take private property for public use is Eminent Domain. The legal procedure to implement the taking is Condemnation. The phrases commonly are used interchangeably.
Statute	Generally Minn. Stat. Chapter 117
Limitations	None
Necessary Parties	"Owners," which includes all persons with an interest in the land
Elements	Land being taken is necessary for a public use or purpose and taking is authorized by law
Burden of Proof	Plaintiff must prove public purpose, necessity and authority; Owner must prove amount of damages due for the taking
Standard of Proof	Preponderance
Defenses	Land not needed, no public use or purpose, too much or too little taken, condemning authority did not negotiate in good faith or considered taking only part but did not get appraisal or negotiate for both part and whole, petition omits land or property right being taken, failure to follow statutory requirements, taking not authorized.
Oddities	Every Condemnation case is initiated by a governmental entity (or quasi-governmental entity e.g. railroad or utility) having the power

of eminent domain. The entity will be represented by an attorney and in our experience, they generally are knowledgeable about the law and procedures.

Judges Van de North and Guthmann prepared an excellent procedural guide found at **Second Judicial District Judicial Policy No. P 13.02, Condemnation Proceedings Handbook.** Any party to the proceedings may appeal the condemnation commissioner's award to the district court and is entitled to a jury trial. Minn. Stat.117.145 and 117.165, Subd. 1. The party appealing the award must file its appeal within 40 days from the date that the report is filed. Minn. Stat. 117.145. The trial is *de novo*, but the condemnation commissioners may be called as witnesses. Minn. Stat. 117.175, Subd. 1.

Special Torrens Note

Notice of Lis Pendens and Final Certificate must be recorded on the Certificate of Title to affect Torrens land. If a good faith purchaser for value takes title without notice of the taking, the condemning authority's rights may be limited or lost. Minn. Stat. 508.25.

A condemnation case is brought as a civil action, not as a Proceeding Subsequent, even if the affected lands are Torrens.

Rule 215 Minn. Gen. R. Prac. does not require Examiner of Titles approval of condemnation orders before presentation to the court.

If the taking is an easement, the Final Certificate remains a memorial on the Certificate of Title. If the taking is in fee, the Final Certificate remains a memorial until a Certificate of Examiner of Titles is issued under Minn. Stat. 508.73, Subd. 1, which directs the Registrar of Titles to issue new Certificates of Title to the condemning authority and owner of the residue parcel for their respective legal descriptions.

Citations

Condemnation cases come before the court in four ways:

The Court makes the initial determination of public purpose or use, necessity and authority, which can be contested and appealed within 60 days after service of the Court's order granting the petition. Minn. Stat. 117.055, Subd. 2(b). If the owner intends to challenge the taking, the objection must be raised at the hearing on the petition. *State v. Wren*, 146 N.W.2d 547 (Minn. 1966);

If the petition requests title and possession to the property before the completion of the condemnation action (referred to as "Quick-Take"), the Court may include such transfer in its order granting the petition, prior to the final award of damages. Minn. Stat. 117.042. The amount of money owed is not at issue in Quick Take because the proper value of the taking will be determined in later proceedings, although the damage amount initially established by the condemning authority must be paid to the owner or deposited with the Court Administrator and can be released to the owner upon order of the Court, which is routinely granted. Minn. Stat. 117.042 details the procedure;

At the initial hearing on the petition, the Court appoints three disinterested Condemnation Commissioners, and at least two alternates, to ascertain and report the amount of damages that will be sustained by the owners from the taking. Minn. Stat. 117.075, Subd. 2. The Court will consider *de novo* in all jury trial appeals from the Commissioner's awards; and

In certain condemnations involving business or farm properties, there are special value rules that apply, such as the right of a business owner to be paid enough to acquire a comparable replacement business property even if it exceeds the amount of damage from the project (Minn. Stat. 117.187), and the right of farmers to elect "Buy the Farm" in power line condemnations (Minn. Stat. 216E.12, Subd. 4). The eligibility of the land being condemned may be contested in a Court proceeding, before the Commissioners have made their damage award.

The word "necessary" means "reasonably necessary or convenient." The 2006 amendments did not overturn prior case law on that point.
State v. Kettleson, 801 N.W. 2d 160 (Minn. 2011)

Condemning authorities often deny that the landowner can object to the petition for failure to include property or a property right. The trial court must rule on these objections.
State v. McAndrews, 175 N.W.2d 492 (Minn. 1970)

2018 update:
The rule at common law was that when government obtains land for a restricted purpose (for park purposes), the landowner retained rights in the land. If the government filed to use the land for the stated purpose, title reverted to the landowner. In addition, the rule at common law was that when government condemns land for a right-of-way, it obtains only an easement.
Fairchild v. City of St. Paul, 49 N.W. 325 (1891)

The old rule was changed by statute. Condemnation can be an easement or in fee simple.
Minn. Stat. 117.215

The old rule was further weakened by case-law. When a Final Certificate states the land was taken "in fee simple for a public park," the words "for a public park" are a statement of the public purpose justifying the taking and thus are merely explanatory, not limiting.
Housing and Redevelopment Authority of City of South Saint Paul v. United Stockyards Corp., 244 N.W.2d 275 (1976).
Piche v. Independent School District No. 621, 634 N.W.2d 193 (Minn. App. 2001).

2019 update:
Lands taken by the state through condemnation for highway purposes, transferred from the state to a municipality to be used for commercial purposes, may not violate the statute requiring the condemning authority to offer the land back to the original owner. Discussion of Minn. Stat. 161.16, Subd 4(b) versus 161.44, Subd. 2.
LaPlant Properties, Inc., v. State of Minnesota and City of Buffalo, A19-0334, unpublished, (Minn. App. 2019)

2021 update:
Entitlement to replacement housing upheld.
In the Matter of Goerisch, unpublished, A20-0939 (Minn. App. 2021)

Contract for Deed and Purchase Agreement Cancellation Primer

1. Under the doctrine of equitable conversion, a definite, non-contingent purchase agreement creates a property interest in the buyer and does not automatically terminate upon default of the buyer. Absent a consensual termination by the parties or a (very rarely used) judicial termination by the court, such a purchase agreement can only be terminated by means of statutory cancellation under Minn. Stat. 559.21 or Minn. Stat. 559.217 (applicable only to residential properties). *Romain v. Pebble Creek Partners*, 310 N.W.2d 118 (Minn. 1981).

2. As a result, both purchase agreements (holding devices) and contracts for deed (seller financing mechanisms) are terminated under the cancellation statutes. Minn. Stat. 559.21 allows cancellation of both contracts for deed (with a typical 60-day notice) and residential and non-residential purchase agreements (with a typical 30-day notice) but only by the seller for the buyer's default. Minn. Stat. 559.217 allows cancellation of only residential purchase agreements upon a 15-day notice by either the seller or the buyer based, under Subd. 3 (cancellation with right to cure), upon a default or an unfulfilled condition which doesn't by the terms of the purchase agreement terminate the purchase agreement or, under Subd. 4 (declaratory cancellation), upon an unfulfilled condition which, by the terms of the purchase agreement, does automatically terminate the purchase agreement.

3. The cancellation notice is served in the same manner as commencement of a civil action upon the buyer (or, in the case of Minn. Stat. 559.217, the seller or buyer and any party holding earnest money) and, in the case of a Contract for Deed, upon any assignees or mortgagees of the contract

purchaser, including holders of tax liens (but not judgment creditors of the purchaser).

4. The effect of the expiration of the cancellation period is to terminate the Contract for Deed or purchase agreement and any property interest in the buyer unless the default is cured or, in the case of Minn. Stat. 559.217, the unfulfilled condition is satisfied during the cancellation period (except in the case of declaratory cancellation) or the served party procures an injunction against the cancellation under Minn. Stat. 559.211.

5. Upon completion of a cancellation, the Contract for Deed seller retains all Contract for Deed payments previously made by the buyer and, with respect to cancellation under the residential purchase agreement statute, the earnest money is delivered to/retained by the party initiating the cancellation notice (except in the case of a counter-cancellation by the other party pursuant to Minn. Stat. 559.217).

6. Upon completion of a cancellation, the buyer loses virtually all claims against the seller, including fraud and other unliquidated damage claims, *Olson v. Northern Pacific Railway*, 148 N.W. 67 (1914), and the seller similarly loses virtually all claims against the buyer, including claims for waste. *Rudnitski v. Seely*, 452 N.W.2d 664 (1990). Exceptions may exist for a buyer's unjust enrichment claim against the seller for plotting unfair advantage, *Brakke v. Hilgers*, 374 N.W.2d 553 (Minn. App. 1985) or a seller's claim against a buyer for personal property, *Rudnitski v. Seely, supra*.

2019 update:

Contract for Deed Seller may owe Contract for Deed Buyer a duty of care even after the Contract for Deed is signed.
Timmons v. Parker, A18-0375, unpublished (Minn. App. 2019)

Contract for Deed – deed in fulfillment not delivered

Summary	Action brought when paid-off Seller fails to deliver a deed in fulfillment of Seller's obligation under a Contract for Deed
Statute	None. Cases generally pled as Specific Performance seeking an Order to deliver the deed but may be Breach of Contract for failure to deliver the deed or Action to Determine Adverse Claims seeking declaration that Buyer is the owner despite Seller's failure to deliver the deed.
Limitations	**Disputed.** Minn. Stat. 541.05, Subd.1 (1) provides six years for contract disputes but applying that to deny an action to clear title seems unfair. **No case law.**
Necessary Parties	Seller (or present holder of Seller's interest, if assigned)
Elements	Contract for Deed outstanding and has not been canceled Buyer has fully performed its obligations under the contract Seller's failure to deliver deed
Burden of Proof	Buyer
Standard of Proof	Preponderance
Defenses	Failure to prove an element

Oddities	The court will typically order the seller to issue a deed upon payment of the purchase price. In that situation, the order should provide that if the seller fails to do so, recording a certified copy of the court's order will have the effect of a conveyance to the buyer under Rule 70 Minn. R. Civ. Pro divesting title from the seller and vesting it in the buyer.
	In some cases, the buyer is withholding the final balloon payment from an uncooperative seller, so the Court should condition its order compelling the deed upon the buyer depositing the final payment with the Court Administrator or a title insurance company pending transfer of title to the buyer.
Special Torrens Note	If the Subject Property is Torrens and the relief sought is a new Certificate of Title in the buyer's name despite the lack of a deed in fulfillment of the Contract for Deed, then arguably the action should be brought as a Proceeding Subsequent, but **there is no case law either way.**
	Rule 215 Minn. Gen. R. Prac. requires an order in a civil case that affects Torrens land to be approved as to form by Examiner of Titles before presentation to court.

Citations
    Good background cases:
        Colstad v. Levine, 67 N.W.2d 648 (1954)
        Gethsemane Lutheran Church v. Zacho, 104 N.W.2d 645 (1960)

Buyer can obtain specific performance against the seller despite the fact that the contract provides that there is no personal recourse against the buyer.
>*Saliterman v. Bigos*, 352 N.W.2d 494 (Minn. App. 1984)

Under Minnesota Title Standard 26, a recorded Contract for Deed remains a cloud on title for 21 years after its initial maturity date or, if there is no stated maturity date, its date of recording. However, a buyer's right to enforce the Contract for Deed may be lost if the seller can prove (by clear and convincing evidence) that the buyer has abandoned the Contract for Deed.
> *Application of Berman,* 247 N.W.2d 405 (1976)
> *Republic Nat. Life Ins. Co. v. Marquette Bank & Trust Co., of Rochester,* 295 N.W.2d 89 (Minn. 1980)

Contract for Deed – enjoin statutory cancellation

Summary	The buyer under a Contract for Deed may seek an injunction to stay the seller's statutory cancellation of the Contract for Deed
Statute	Minn. Stat. 559.211
Limitations	Buyer must first have commenced a civil action and must meet requirements of Rule 65 of Rules of Civil Procedure and *Dahlberg* factors for injunctive relief (below). Cancellation period is typically 60 days, so Buyer must make its motion prior to expiration of that 60-day period.
Necessary Parties	Buyer and Seller, but the attorney authorized in the cancellation notice to accept payment is designated the seller's agent for service of process in the action to restrain cancellation. Minn. Stat. 559.21, Subd. 8.
Elements	Seller is not entitled to cancel the Contract for Deed. Buyer may rely on any defense to cancellation.
Burden of Proof	Buyer (moving party)
Standard of Proof	Preponderance
Defenses	Seller defending against the motion for injunction must show Seller is entitled to cancel the contract because Buyer is in default. Partial cure (usually payment) waives cancellation

Real Estate Reference Guide for Judges

Oddities	Court may grant TRO without requiring security – see below.

Post-injunction grace period: If TRO or injunction is granted, contract cancels no earlier than 15 days after TRO or injunction is dissolved. Minn. Stat. 559.211, Subd. 1.

Until recently, Buyer was required to assert all defenses **during** the cure period or lose them. Sellers may cite these cases:
    Thomey v. Stewart, 391 N.W.2d 533 (Minn. App. 1986)
    Nowicki v.Benson Properties, 402 N.W.2d 205 (Minn. App. 1987)
    Henry v. Schultz, 408 N.W.2d 635 (Minn. App. 1987)

However, Minn. Stat. 559.211, Subd. 2 was amended in 2013 to overturn that absolute requirement. Those cases are no longer controlling, but some defenses not asserted during the cure period can be lost – see below.

A Contract for Deed need not be recorded to be canceled.
    Van Riper v. Roy, A15-0844 unpublished (Minn. App. 2016) |
| Special Torrens Note | Case may be brought as civil action. Proceeding Subsequent is not required because an action for an injunction does not seek to alter the Certificate of Title. If the injunction is not granted and the Contract for |

Deed is canceled, the memorials of the Contract for Deed and the Notice of Cancellation remain on the Certificate of Title until removed by order in a Proceeding Subsequent or by Examiner's Directive (Minn. Stat. 508.58, Subd. 5).

Rule 215 Minn. Gen. R. Prac. requires an order in a civil case that affects Torrens land to be approved as to form by Examiner of Titles before presentation to court.

Citations

Under the injunction statute, Buyer may rely on any matter that would constitute a defense to the cancellation. Minn. Stat. 559.211, Subd. 1. For example, payment by Buyer, non-material default, defects in the cancellation notice, waiver by Seller, or fraud, misrepresentation or other wrongful acts by Seller are defenses. Because the effect of a completed cancellation may be termination of Buyer's interest (and the buyer should not have to later litigate post-cancellation at the peril of being wrong), an injunction may be granted against cancellation even where the buyer claims that it is not in default, *Craigmile v. Sorenson*, 62 N.W.2d 846 (1954) or where the defense, if successful, would survive statutory cancellation, *Jeddeloh v. Altman*, 247 N.W. 512 (1933) (claim that Contract for Deed was equitable mortgage). Also, if Buyer is uncertain as to amount to cure, injunctive relief is appropriate as guessing wrong can be fatal.

In evaluating requests for injunctive relief, the court will consider the five factors set forth in *Dahlberg Bros., Inc. v. Ford Motor Co.*, 137 N.W.2d 314 (1965):

i. The nature of the relationship of the parties prior to the dispute;
ii. The harm likely to be suffered by either party if the injunctive relief is granted or denied;
iii. The likelihood that one party or the other will ultimately prevail at trial;
iv. Public policy considerations, if any; and
v. The administrative burden on the court if the temporary injunctive relief is granted.

Due to the fact that the harm from a failure to grant the injunctive relief will often mean the loss of all claims by the buyer under the *Olson* rule (mentioned below), courts have tended to grant injunctive relief as long as the buyer's claim seems meritorious.

A trial court may not enjoin cancellation of a Contract for Deed unless an underlying cause of action exists.
Smith v. Spitzenberger, 363 N.W.2d 470 (Minn. App. 1985)

Misstatements of the amount due on the contract (which the buyer is presumed to know) and minor variations from the statutory form of the cancellation notice do not invalidate a cancellation.
In re Edina Dev. Corp., 370 B.R. 894 (Bankr. D. Minn. 2007)

Although precedent is not clear, there is authority that an "immaterial" default of one payment under the Contract for Deed may not justify cancellation.
Coddon v. Youngkrantz, 562 N.W.2d 39 (Minn. App. 1997)

Under the injunction statute, the court may grant a temporary restraining order without the buyer posting a bond, but the

buyer must post a bond or future contract payments as a prerequisite to an injunction.
>Seger v. DeGardner, 355 N.W.2d 465 (Minn. App. 1984)

Courts have been upheld for both requiring, *Eide v. Bierbaum*, 472 N.W.2d 193 (Minn. App. 1991), and not requiring, *Carlson v. Mixell*, 412 N.W.2d 771 (Minn. App. 1987), security for pre-injunction payments.

For a period of time, cases such as *Thomey v. Stewart*, 391 N.W.2d 533 (Minn. App. 1986) (defense of waiver lost due to failure to timely procure injunction against cancellation) and others held that all defenses to cancellation were lost if the buyer failed to procure an injunction during the cancellation period. Minn. Stat. 559.211, Subd. 2 was amended in 2013 to overturn that absolute requirement. However, many defenses, such as a claim of fraud against Seller or other claims not directly related to the mechanics of statutory cancellation, do not survive the cancellation period and will be lost if no injunction is procured prior to the running of the cancellation period. *Olsen v. Northern Pacific Railway*, 148 N.W. 67 (1914) and other cases.

See also: Roberts, 25 Minnesota Practice Real Estate Law Section 6:22 (citation not verified).

2021 update:
>Seller initiated cancellation of a contract for deed for failure to make payments; Buyer sought an injunction claiming the contract for deed terms were ambiguous; court found the terms were not ambiguous and granted summary judgment to Seller.
>>*Pexsa v. Disabled American Veterans of Minnesota Foundation*, unpublished, A19-2041 (Minn. App. 2021)

Minn. Stat. 559.211, Subd 1 provides that the court is authorized to issue a temporary restraining order to enjoin further proceedings in an action to cancel a purchase agreement. A TRO issued before the action has been filed is void. Whether the void TRO "stopped the clock" running on the statutory cancelation period, was remanded.
Martsching v. Zillmer, unpublished, A20-0880 (Minn. App. 2021)

2023 update:

Ambiguous terms in a contract for deed regarding purchase price and responsibility for septic upgrades preclude summary judgment in favor of Seller's statutory cancellation.
Feltus v. Niemala, unpublished, A22-0673, (Minn. App. 2023)

Seller attempted to serve Notice of Cancellation on Buyer at his residence by handing to and leaving with a woman who identified herself as Buyer's mother and stated she lived there but who refused to accept service and directed the process server to leave the notice in the door. Buyer alleged defective service because the house is a duplex and his mother lived in the other half; thus, she was not "residing therein" for purposes of substitute service. Held: a material issue of fact exists whether service was proper.
Hagle v. Gossett Properties LLC, unpublished, A22-0135 (Minn. App. 2022)

Constitutional Lien

Summary	The homestead is normally exempt from collection; this is an exception
Statute	None: arises under Article 1, Section 12, Minnesota Constitution
Limitation	Requires judgment arising from a separate cause of action (e.g. breach of contract, *quantum meruit*, unjust enrichment)
Necessary Parties	Landowner of record, lien holders, occupants
Elements	Work done or materials furnished in construction, repair or improvement of real property, by direct contract with the owner.
Burden of Proof	Person claiming the lien
Standard of Proof	Preponderance
Defenses	No direct contract with owner Value of work
Oddities	Technically, a homestead lien is not a separate cause of action, it provides an exception to the homestead exemption so an underlying judgment obtained on other grounds can be enforced against the homestead. The common law "constitutional lien" for improvement to real estate often is pled as an alternative basis for relief in mechanic's lien

foreclosures when the mechanic's lien claimant may have failed to follow the statutory requirements to perfect a mechanic's lien and isn't entitled to one. A "Constitutional Lien" does not require a lien statement recorded in the title records nor pre-lien notice.

Order portion should include statement "Judgment is a lien on [insert legal description of homestead]."

Unlike mechanic's lien, there is no authority for the court to award interest or attorney's fees on a constitutional lien.

Special Torrens Note	Rule 215 Minn. Gen. R. Prac. requires an order in a civil case that affects Torrens land to be approved as to form by Examiner of Titles before presentation to court.
Citations	*ServiceMaster of St. Cloud v. GAB Business Services, Inc.*, 544 N.W.2d 302 (Minn. 1996)

Easements

Summary	Action to declare whether an easement exists or clarify its terms (example, driveway is shared, but nothing is in writing)
Statute	Varies with legal theory, usually pled as declaratory judgment under Minn. Stat. Chapter 555 when brought to establish or clarify an easement; or as action to determine adverse claims under Minn. Stat. Chapter 559 when brought to remove from title or enjoin use of an easement
Limitations	Minn. Stat. 541.023 (40-year law – but does not apply to Torrens or to persons still in actual possession of the easement); 541.02 (15-year law)
Necessary Parties	Landowner of record, lien holders, persons using or claiming rights to land
Definitions	*Appurtenant Easement*: benefits a specific parcel of land ("Benefitted Parcel") and burdens another ("Burdened Parcel" or "Servient Estate"). Runs with the land and binds future owners. *Easement in Gross*: usually personal, does not run with land, usually not transferable. *Negative Easement:* restricts otherwise legal use (example: building restriction to maintain air and light or view)
Elements	Varies with legal theory. Every order regarding an easement must state the legal description of benefitted and burdened parcels

so the order can be recorded in the Tract Index and on the affected Certificates of Title.

Easement by Agreement. Must be in writing (Statute of Frauds, Minn. Stat. 513.04). Location, width, use, persons benefitted determined by parties' intent.

Easement by Estoppel: Landowner represented to the buyer that there was access, a representation on which the buyer reasonably relied to her detriment. Landowner is estopped from denying the easement. Location determined by court.

Easement dedicated by plat. Minn. Stat. Chapter 505.021, Subd. 7. Must be shown on plat, mentioned in dedication clause, approved by municipality and recorded. Width = dimensions on plat.

Implied Easement: Usually arises from landlocked parcel. Two types of implied easements:

> Quasi-easement: one owner owned all the land, sold part, failed to include an access easement; the easement is implied in the sale. Location determined by court.
>
> Easement by Necessity: **See: Streets and Access – Easement by Necessity, below.**

Nathan Bissonette

Easement for right-of-way by statutory dedication. **See: Streets and Access – Statutory User, below.**

Cartway. **See: Streets and Access – Cartway, below.**

Easement for right-of-way by common law dedication: **See: Streets and Access – Common Law Dedication, below.**

Prescriptive Easement. **See: Streets and Access – Prescriptive Easement, below.**

Burden of Proof	Plaintiff
Standard of Proof	Preponderance; except prescriptive easement, which is clear and convincing
Defenses	Easement is no longer enforceable because of abandonment or merger; easement is not in the claimed location; use exceeds permitted scope of activities.
	If an easement claim is based on prescription, then defenses to adverse possession (permission, lack of continuity) could apply.
	Easement is more than 40 years old and no longer in use, Minn. Stat. 541.023 (does not apply to Torrens).
	Minn. Stat 500.20 (30-year law) expressly refers to "covenants, conditions, restrictions" but not to easements, so it doesn't apply.

Real Estate Reference Guide for Judges

Oddities

If mortgage lender did not consent to a junior easement given by landowner, the easement is extinguished by foreclosure. *In re Crablex, Inc.,* 762 N.W.2d 247 (Minn. App. 2009). This rule might not apply to an involuntary easement (example: prescriptive easement).

Easements survive a tax forfeiture sale. Minn. Stat. 282.01, Subd. 6

Special Torrens Note

Easements can be litigated in an Initial Registration action brought under Minn. Stat. 508.06.

If the land burdened by the easement is Torrens and the requested relief seeks to alter the Certificate of Title (for example, by removing an easement), the case must be brought as a Proceeding Subsequent under Minn. Stat. 508.71, Subd. 2.

If the Torrens land is benefitted by the easement, and the easement rights have been registered, the case must be brought as a Proceeding Subsequent under Minn. Stat. 508.71, Subd. 2.

If the Torrens land is benefitted by the easement, but the easement rights have not been registered, the case can be brought as a civil action.

Rule 215 Minn. Gen. R. Prac. requires an order in a civil case that affects Torrens land to be approved as to form by Examiner of Titles before presentation to court.

Nathan Bissonette

Citations
See each legal theory, above.

Mere failure to use an easement does not necessarily extinguish it.
Richards Asphalt Co. v. Bunge Corp., 399 N.W.2d 188 (Minn. App. 1987)

Elements of Implied Easement discussed.
Nerland v. Kristy Lee Marie Barsch, A16-0318 unpublished (Minn. App. 2016)

2018 update:
Street automatically includes utility easements.
Carter v. Nw. Tel. Exch. Co., 63 N.W. 111 (Minn. 1895)
Minneapolis Gas Co. v. Zimmerman, 91 N.W.2d 642 (Minn. 1958)

2019 update:
The natural right to surface water flowage or drainage is not a true easement. Elements of easements by implication, prescription, necessity and estoppel explained. Statute of limitations applied.
Aeshliman v. Smisek, A18-0752, unpublished (Minn. App. 2018)

Shared driveway easement interpreted, injunction denied, costs awarded.
Athanasakoupolous v. Bogart, A18-0045, unpublished (Minn. App. 2018)

To create an express easement, the granting language must be unambiguous. Here, Mother's deed to Daughter created a roadway easement for Mother's benefit but did not create a reciprocal roadway easement for Daughter. The easement

runs with the land. Daughter's claim for an implied easement roadway was remanded.
>*Kalahar-Grissom v. Stroschein,* A18-1135, unpublished (Minn. App. 2019)

2020 update:
Terms of an express parking easement over appurtenant land control the use of the easement and are not extinguished by failure to mention the easement in a conveyance deed.
>*KK-Five Corporation v. Groveland Terrace Condominium Owners' Association,* unpublished, A18-2001, (Minn. App).

A license conveys a revocable privilege to do an act upon the land of another; an easement conveys an irrevocable right to keep doing it.
>*LTI 9500, LLC v. Security Warehouse/5th Avenue Lofts Association,* unpublished, A18-1991 (Minn. App. 2018).

Long-standing quarry access road deemed prescriptive easement. Action to determine the easement is not thwarted by Town Board's willingness to provide cart-way.
>*Grannes v. Red Cedar of Yellow Medicine, Inc.,* unpublished, A04-1264 (Minn. App 2005).

Deed reformed to include an omitted easement.
>*Isanti Pines Tree Farm LLC v. Swanson,* unpublished, A19-0749, A19-1585 (Minn. App. 2020).

2021 update:
Easements on Lake Minnetonka interpreted.
>*Dunkley v. Hueler, et. al.,* unpublished, A19-2047 (Minn. App. 2020)

The elements to prove a prescriptive easement are the same as for adverse possession except "use" is substituted for

"possession," viz. Open Use, Continuous Use, Hostile Use, etc.
> *Saba v. Anderson*, unpublished, A20-1291 (Minn. App. 2021)

An easement "in gross" is the right to use another's property that is personal and revocable. An "appurtenant" easement is runs with the land and therefore passes to subsequent owners. The determination depends on the parties' intent when the easement is created. Expert witness testimony was properly excluded because the expert would have testified about the legal meaning of terms in the 1941 quitclaim deed which would not have aided the court in deciding the legal issue before it. The district court excluded historical use testimony because it was not relevant to the intent of the parties when the easement was drafted, but the Court of Appeals remanded because the scope of the easement was ambiguous and historical use testimony was relevant to determining that scope.
> *Jensen v. Rindelaub*, unpublished, A20-1084 (Minn. App. 2021)

2022 update:

An easement deed was given in 2013 for "public road, drainage utility purposes." A second easement deed was given in 2016 which shifted the easement southward and reduced its width from 66 to 40 feet but did not specify uses. When the buyer of the burdened parcel expressed a desire to build a home, the Grantor of the easement objected that the easement no longer permitted utilities, only a 40-foot road. The trial court found the combination of deeds was ambiguous as to the parties' intent. To resolve the ambiguity, the trial court made detailed findings regarding the historical use of the easement, the current and previous deeds describing the easement, and the purpose of modifying the easement. The court of appeals upheld those findings.
> *Bexell v. Brand,* unpublished, A21-1302 (Minn. App. 2022)

When a driveway easement was granted, it reached a public road. After the public road was vacated, affected property owners entered into a Road and Utility Easement Agreement. A later owner reconfigured boundaries and intended to use the easement for access to a newly created parcel. Good analysis of 'expanding the use of an easement' claim.
> *Dunkley v. Hueler*, unpublished A19-2047 (Minn. App. 2020)

The Burdened Property owner obstructed an easement. The Benefitted Property owner sued to enforce the easement rights including claims that the obstructions were a private nuisance. Court analyzed what constitutes a nuisance, scope of easement and permissible infringements, and then balanced the interests of the parties.
> *Bradley v. Haislet,* unpublished, A20-1207 (Minn. App. 2021)

2023 update:

Not a new case, found while researching a street case. The plat said, "Excepting the easterly fifteen feet of said Lot A, which is reserved for a foot and bicycle path for the benefit at all times of any and all of the owners of any of the land in said East Shore Park." Held: The word "excepting" was construed to mean "granted" to effectuate the manifest intent of the Grantor to create the easement. Fee title to the land under the easement belonged to the Grantee, subject to the easement.
> *Aldrich v. Soucheray*, 133 Minn. 382, 158 N. W. 637 (Minn. 1916)

Another old case for the same point. Deed conveyed a parcel 33 x 90 "excepting and reserving therefrom a strip of land 10 feet wide and 33 feet long, across the rear or inner end of said 90 feet, for an alley." Held: The phrase "excepting and reserving" did not indicate the Grantor retained fee title to the

strip. Instead, fee title to the strip vested in Grantee, subject to an easement for alley over the strip. Grantee owes the taxes on the strip of land under the alley.
    Winston v. Johnson, 45 N.W. 958 (Minn. 1890)

Buyer and Seller signed a purchase agreement which noted the existence of a telecommunications easement set to expire in 2026. Later, Seller gave an extended easement lasting nearly 100 years. Held: The doctrine of equitable conversion provides that once the parties have executed a binding contract for the sale of real estate, Seller must preserve the condition of title as it existed at the time of the contract and is precluded from extending the easement.
    Howard v. Sun Trust Financial LLC, unpublished, A21-1634 (Minn. App. 2022)

Developer split a large lot into two smaller lots, A (which had access to a public right of way) and B (which was landlocked). An access easement across A for the benefit of B was not recorded. 15 years later, Developer sought an easement by necessity over A's land for the benefit of B. Held: The easement is necessary to the beneficial enjoyment of B, but Developer's claim is barred by laches and unclean hands. Lot B remains landlocked and undeveloped.
    In re Bacchus, unpublished, A22-0610 (Minn. App. 2023)

Owner of property burdened by easement sought to have the easement terminated because the benefitted property had not continuously occupied the easement (and therefore it expired under the Marketable Title Act); and because the benefitted property owner impermissibly expanded the use of the easement. Denied.
    In re Mojtaba Sharifkhani, unpublished, A22-0617 (Minn. App. 2022)

Access easement benefited three properties with shared road access burdened property. Easement provides Grantor or Grantee may improve the easement without obligating the other party to assist in payment. Burdened and two Benefitted owners agreed to split cost of improvements. Burdened failed to pay his share and removed crushed rock from the road to other lands. Held: Burdened landowner could not be forced to pay under the easement agreement but the later agreement to split improvement costs was a new contract which he breached, and removing the crushed rock unjustly enriched him.

Neiman v. Sandin, unpublished, A22-0764 (Minn. App. 2023)

Equitable subrogation

Summary	Action based in equity to adjust priority among creditor; one steps into another's shoes (example: mortgage lender paid off contract-for-deed and gets that lien's recording priority date)
Statute	None. Pled as Declaratory Judgment under Chapter 555
Limitations	No statute of limitations; equitable defenses such as laches may apply
Necessary Parties	Landowner of record, lien holders, occupants

Elements	Party seeking subrogation has:
	    paid the debt of another, and
	    acted under a justifiable or excusable mistake of fact, and
	    injury to innocent party will result if not subrogated

Burden of Proof	Plaintiff
Standard of Proof	Preponderance
Defenses	Failure to prove element; equitable defenses (laches, negligence, unclean hands, etc.)
Oddities	Subrogation commonly is sought when a lender gives a loan to pay off a Contract for Deed or prior mortgage, then discovers encumbrances such as mechanic's liens, state

Real Estate Reference Guide for Judges

Special Torrens Note	or federal tax liens, judgments or intervening mortgages that have priority over the new loan. The new lender will seek an Order giving it the priority position of the Contract for Deed as against the other lien holders. If the land is Torrens and the relief sought is to change the priority of encumbrances shown on the Certificate of Title (for example, in anticipation of a mortgage foreclosure), the action should be brought as a Proceeding Subsequent. Rule 215 Minn. Gen. R. Prac. requires an order in a civil case that affects Torrens land to be approved as to form by Examiner of Titles before presentation to court.

Citations

Under equitable subrogation, when a person has discharged the debt of another with respect to real property, that person may be substituted in place of a prior encumbrancer and treated as an equitable assignee of the lien. In other words, that person may be substituted to the rights and position of the prior creditor.
    First Nat'l Bank of Menahga v. Schunk, 276 N.W. 290 (Minn. 1937)

"Although [equitable] subrogation is a highly favored doctrine, it is not an absolute right, but rather, one that depends on the equities and attending facts and circumstances of each case."
    Universal Title Ins. Co. v. United States, 942 F.2d 1311, 1315 (8th Cir.1991)

Equitable subrogation will not be applied when the parties' equities are equal or rights are unclear.
    S. Sur. Co. v. Tessum, 228 N.W. 326 (Minn. 1929)

Equitable subrogation "will be applied in the interest of substantial justice ... where one party has provided funds used to discharge another's obligations if (a) the party seeking subrogation has acted under a justifiable or excusable mistake of fact and (b) injury to innocent parties will otherwise result."
    Carl H. Peterson Co. v. Zero Estates, 261 N.W.2d 346 (Minn.1977)

An unexplained 38-day delay in resubmitting a mortgage to the county recorder's office for recording after the mortgage was returned by the county recorder's office unrecorded is not a justifiable or excusable mistake of fact that warrants applying equitable subrogation.
    Citizens State Bank v. Raven Trading Partners, Inc., 786 N.W.2d 274 (Minn. 2010)

Real Estate Reference Guide for Judges

Foreclosure by Action (of a mortgage)

Summary	Action for breach of contract for default under the mortgage with order to sell land to satisfy the judgment or obtain deficiency judgment against Borrower.
Statute	Minn. Stat. Chapter 581
Limitations	Minn. Stat. 541.03 – action must be brought within 15 years of maturity
Necessary Parties	Landowner of record, lien holders, occupants, homeowner's association if land in CIC, taxing authorities
Elements	Default under the terms of the Mortgage (generally non-payment)
Burden of Proof	Present Mortgage holder
Standard of Proof	Preponderance
Defenses	No valid debt; no valid mortgage; not in default; usury. "Show me the note" is NOT a defense, see below.
Oddities	Borrower has signed a Mortgage pledging real estate as collateral for a loan evidenced by a Promissory Note. When Borrower fails to repay, Lender sues for breach of contract on the Note and foreclosure of the mortgage. Court enters judgment for dollar amount on the contract claim, then directs the Sheriff to sell the land that was pledged as collateral to satisfy the judgment. Sale procedures same as

Version 7.1   July 1, 2023

Foreclosure by Advertisement, Chapter 580, but must be confirmed by the court.

Court enters Order Confirming Sale, applies proceeds of sale to underlying judgment, calculates deficiency amount to be entered as personal judgment. Sheriff files Certificate of Sale in land records. Redemption period starts with Order Confirming Sale.

This is really a breach of contract claim, the foreclosure is merely a procedure to collect the resulting judgment; therefore, the primary purpose of the action is not to alter a Certificate of Title, so this is not a "Torrens" case and, a Report of Examiner is not needed.

Foreclosure by Action is sometimes brought because of mortgage defects (faulty legal description, no power of sale, mortgage not recorded). Those mortgages still can be foreclosed, but it must be done by action, not by advertisement.

Under current case-law, Foreclosure by Advertisement requires strict compliance with the statute, but Foreclosure by Action does not.

Special rules apply to Agricultural Land, example: Minn. Stat. 582.31 and Chapter 583.

Special Torrens Note	Rule 215 Minn. Gen. R. Prac. which requires an order in a civil case that affects Torrens land to be approved as to form by Examiner of

Real Estate Reference Guide for Judges

Titles before presentation to court, does **not** apply to Foreclosure by Action. Title will not transfer without an Examiner's Directive issued under Minn. Stat. 508.58, Subd. 2.

Citations

"Show me the note" is not a defense. The holder of legal title to a mortgage can foreclose by action without showing that it also holds the promissory note associated with the mortgage.
JPMorgan Chase Bank, N.A. v. Erlandson, 821 N.W.2d 600 (Minn. App. 2012)

The reasons for requiring strict compliance with statutes in Foreclosure by Advertisement do not apply to Foreclosure by Action. The Order Confirming Sale has the effect of a judgment and cannot be collaterally attacked.
Scott v. Hay, 97 N.W. 106 (Minn. 1903)

Foreclosure by Action is the procedure to be used when foreclosure by Advertisement is not available.
Soufal v. Griffith, 198 N.W. 807 (Minn. 1924)

A void attempt to foreclose by advertisement does not destroy the lien of the mortgage or cut off the right to resort to Foreclosure by Action.
Rogers v. Benton, 38 NW. 765 (Minn. 1888)

A lender is entitled to a deficiency judgment in a Foreclosure by Action where the redemption period is six months.
Norwest Bank Hastings, NA v. Franzmeier, 355 N.W.2d 431 (Minn. App. 1984)

The Court may order a farm sold as one parcel despite Minn. Stat. 582.042 and without providing the court the legal descriptions of the tracts to be sold separately in a Foreclosure by Action.

Nathan Bissonette

Roseland v. Wentzell, 864 N.W.2d 356 (Minn. App. 2015). **NOTE: this holding is controversial but is still good law.**

2021 update:
If the amount received at Sheriff's Sale is greater than the amount due on the judgment, the surplus shall be brought into court for the benefit of the mortgagor. Minn. Stat. 581.06.
   SW Partners, LLC v. Trade Center Property, LLC, unpublished, A20-0773 (Minn. App. 2021)

Real Estate Reference Guide for Judges

Foreclosure by Advertisement (of a mortgage)

Summary	Non-judicial proceeding to sell land for default under the Mortgage in lieu of payment on the Promissory Note. Court sees when challenged.
Statute	Minn. Stat. Chapter 580 (foreclosure procedures); 559 (determine adverse claims); and 555 (declaratory judgment);
Limitations	Minn. Stat. 541.03 (15 years after maturity); 582.25 (Curative Act); and 582.26
Necessary Parties	Landowner of record, junior lien holders entitled to notice, occupants
Elements	Depends on the default claimed
Burden of Proof	Plaintiff
Standard of Proof	Preponderance
Defenses	No debt owed, not in default, no valid mortgage, usury, Lender failed to follow statutory foreclosure procedures (strict compliance is required)
Oddities	A Sheriff's Certificate is *prima facie* evidence for a rebuttable presumption that all requirements of law have been complied with, and after the redemption period has expired, is prima facie evidence of title in the name of the purchaser at the sale.

For abstract land, lenders rarely bring an action to validate a foreclosure; usually, the action is brought by borrowers challenging the validity of the foreclosure which is pled as an Action to Determine Adverse Claims under Chapter 559 alleging that the lender acquired no interest in the land by its pretended foreclosure, or a Declaratory Judgment under Chapter 555 alleging that the foreclosure is void and is a slander of title.

Special rules apply to Agricultural Land, example: Minn. Stat. 582.31 and Chapter 583.

Foreclosure challenges must be separate action from eviction.

Special
Torrens Note   Any action arising from foreclosure of Torrens land must be brought as a Proceeding Subsequent. The requirement is jurisdictional; failure is fatal.

Citations

Foreclosure by Advertisement requires strict compliance with statutory procedures.
    Jackson v. Mortgage Electronic Registration Systems, Inc., 770 N.W.2d 487 (Minn. 2009)

Failure to strictly comply renders the purported foreclosure void, upon borrower's timely objection. No showing of prejudice is required.

Real Estate Reference Guide for Judges

Ruiz v. 1st Fidelity Loan Servicing, LLC, 829 N.W.2d 53 (Minn. 2013)

After a Foreclosure by Advertisement affecting Torrens land, Proceedings Subsequent must be brought to adjudicate the validity of the foreclosure to obtain a clean Certificate of Title.
Minn. Stat. 508.58

Any action arising from Foreclosure by Advertisement affecting Torrens land – to confirm the foreclosure or to challenge it – must be brought as a Proceeding Subsequent. This requirement is jurisdictional and failure is fatal.
Phillips v. Dolphin, 776 N.W.2d 755 (Minn. App. 2009); Minn. Stat. 508.58, Subd. 2; Rule 215 Minn. Gen. R. Prac.

"Show me the note" is not a defense to foreclosure by advertisement. The holder of legal title to a mortgage can foreclose by advertisement without showing that it also holds the promissory note associated with the mortgage.
Jackson v. Mortgage Electronic Registration Systems, Inc., 770 N.W.2d 487 (Minn. 2009)

An eviction action is a summary proceeding intended to adjudicate the limited question of who has a present possessory right to a property. *Deutsche Bank Nat'l Trust Co. v. Hanson*, 841 N.W.2d 161, 164 (Minn. App. 2014) . . . "Parties generally may not litigate related claims in an eviction proceeding," but defendants may "raise defenses and counterclaims that fit within the limited scope of an eviction proceeding." *Hansen*, at 164. Challenges to the validity of the mortgage or foreclosure process may be raised in a separate proceeding, in which the party raising the challenges may seek a stay of the eviction action. *AMRESCO Residential Mortg. Corp. v. Stange*, 631 N.W.2d 444, 445-46 (Minn. App. 2001); *see also Real Estate Equity Strategies, LLC v.*

Jones, 720 N.W.2d 352, 359-60 (Minn. App. 2006) (identifying remedies a tenant may pursue outside of an eviction action).

S3 Holdings, LLC v. Niosi, A14-1470 unpublished (Minn. App. 2015)

2018 update:

The phrase "separate and distinct farms or tract" from Minn. Stat. 580.08 was litigated. Lender may sell mortgaged property in a single foreclosure sale because the mortgaged property did not consist of "separate and distinct tracts" even though it consisted of four separate platted lots and four separate property tax parcels.
Leeco, Inc. v. Cornerstone Bank, 898 N.W.2d 653 (Minn. App. 2017)

2020 update:
Property did not meet definition of "single family owner-occupied" so failure to give required notice under Minn. Stat. 580.04 did not void foreclosure.
Boelter v. Steinert, unpublished, A19-1151 (Minn. App. 2020).

Foreclosure by advertisement requires strict compliance with the statute. Failure to state the correct redemption period in the notice of foreclosure renders the foreclosure void, without a showing of prejudice by the mortgagor.
Larsen v. Wells Fargo Bank, NA, unpublished, A19-0952 (Minn. App. 2020)

2021 update:
Home foreclosed by advertisement; owner's redemption period expired without redemption by owner; junior creditor redeemed; owner brought action to set aside foreclosure for failure to give proper notice and to recover title from redeeming junior creditor and its successor in interest. Held: mailed notice is proper under Minn.

Stat. 580.032, Subd. 4. After the owner's redemption period expires without redemption by owner, owner lacks standing to assert claims against redeeming junior creditor and its successor in interest.
Anderson v. MidFirst Bank, et. al., unpublished, A20-1056 (Minn. App. 2021)

Inverse Condemnation

Summary	Action brought to force governmental unit to pay for property rights already taken by other action (example, airport zoning ordinance, flooding as result of government action) but not paid for in condemnation action
Statute	Minn. Stat. 117.045; Minn. Stat. Chapter 586, Petition for Writ of Mandamus seeking to compel condemnation must be filed.
Limitations	15 years from actual physical taking; 6 years from taking of access or other non-physical property right, including "regulatory taking."
Necessary Parties	Government unit that did the alleged taking
Elements	Government took property rights without just compensation
Burden of Proof	Plaintiff
Standard of Proof	Preponderance
Defenses	No "compensable" taking occurred
Oddities	"Inverse Condemnation" is not a cause of action but a descriptive phrase. Normally, when the government wants to take land, it commences a condemnation case. Where the landowner claims the government took rights without paying for them, the remedy sought is compensation, but the case is procedurally backwards, hence, inverse condemnation.

Real Estate Reference Guide for Judges

Regulatory takings (such as zoning ordinances) normally don't trigger compensation unless the regulations are so severe they leave the owner with no economically viable use of the land. Airport zoning cases are a special subset with different standards.

Revocation of a permit or license is not a compensable taking.

Prevailing landowner may receive attorney's fees.

Special Torrens Note

The relief primarily requested is money, similar to a condemnation action, so this proceeding need not be brought as a Proceeding Subsequent.

Rule 215 Minn. Gen. R. Prac., which requires an order in a civil case that affects Torrens land to be approved as to form by Examiner of Titles before presentation to court, does **not** apply to these actions.

Citations

15 years from actual physical taking; 6 years from taking of access or other non-physical property right, including "regulatory taking."

Beer v. Minnesota Power & Light Co., 400 N.W.2d 732 (Minn. 1987)
Kottschade v. City of Rochester, 760 N.W.2d 342 (Minn. App. 2009)

Procedurally, the Court receives a petition for Writ of Mandamus and issues an "alternative" writ requiring the government to initiate condemnation proceedings or, in the alternative, to show cause as to why the court should not issue a Writ of Mandamus. Minn. Stat. 586.02 and 586.03. While Minn. Stat. 586.06 -.08 seems to require that the government file an answer, with the case then proceeding as a normal civil action, it has been interpreted to allow the government to present evidence at the show-cause hearing without filing an answer, where there are no facts in dispute, no question of law requiring additional evidence and no prejudice results to petitioner.

>*Popp v. County of Winona*, 430 N.W.2d 19 (Minn. App. 1988)

Revocation of a permit or license is not a taking.

>*Khan v. Minneapolis City Council*, A14-0455, unpublished (Minn. App. 2014)

Prevailing landowner may receive attorney's fees. Minn. Stat. 117.045
Regulatory takings (such as zoning ordinances) don't trigger compensation unless the regulations are so severe they leave the owner with no economically viable use of the land. The landmark cases are:

>*Lucas v. South Carolina Coastal Council*, 505 US 1003 (1992)
>*First English Evangelical Lutheran Church of Glendale v. County of Los Angeles, California*, 482 US 304 (1987)
>*Lingle v. Chevron*, 544 US 528 (2005)

Airport zoning cases are a special subset of regulatory takings:

>*McShane v. City of Faribault*, 292 N.W.2d 253 (Minn. 1980)
>*DeCook v. Rochester International Airport Joint Zoning Board*, 811 N.W.2d 610 (Minn. 2012)

Real Estate Reference Guide for Judges

O'Neill v. City of Bloomington, A13-1114, unpublished (Minn. App. 2014)
Interstate Cos v. City of Bloomington, 790 N.W.2d 409 (Minn. App. 2010)

A question frequently arises in the case of onerous requirements or excessive exactions in connection with the land use and zoning or subdivision approvals which can constitute a form of condemnation. See, for example: *Country Joe, Inc. v. City of Eagan*, 560 N.W.2d 681 (Minn. 1997)

2021 update:
Owners of a condominium apartment located across the alley from a new office building suffered increased alley traffic, increased noise and fumes from traffic, increased odors from diesel generators, fumes from air ventilators into the alley and employees smoking in the alley, increased light from headlights and overhead lighting and decreased privacy. None of these are more intrusive than suffered by an average community member living in downtown Duluth would reasonably anticipate and therefore are not compensable takings. Condo owners' rights under implied easements for light, air and view over the alley only extend to the alley, not to land on the other side of the alley.

Bystedt v. City of Duluth, unpublished, A20-1170 (Minn. App. 2021)

2023 update:

Port Authority of the City of St. Paul (Buyer) purchased a parking ramp under threat of condemnation but never made a payment to Metro Real Estate Services (Seller). The lender foreclosed. Held: Seller could not bring a claim for inverse condemnation against the

Port Authority because Seller was no longer the owner and therefore was not deprived of practical enjoyment of the property.
> *Wells Fargo Bank v. Port Auth. of St. Paul,* unpublished, A22-1226 (Minn. App. 2023)

Real Estate Reference Guide for Judges

Jurisdiction and Venue

The maxim that District Courts are courts of general jurisdiction is not entirely accurate.

> Personal jurisdiction: Minnesota district courts have personal jurisdiction over persons residing in the state or having sufficient minimum contacts with this state to support long-arm jurisdiction.
>
> Subject Matter jurisdiction: Some courts have limited specific subject-matter jurisdiction. For example, one could not obtain a divorce by filing a Petition for Dissolution of Marriage in Housing Court.

Special Torrens Note: If the relief sought **primarily** involves altering a Certificate of Title, (example, an action to adjudicate the validity of the foreclosure of a mortgage on Torrens land), the case must be brought as a Proceeding Subsequent so the Examiner of Titles can file a Report of Examiner. This is jurisdictional: Bringing the action as a Declaratory Judgment, Quiet Title or Action to Determine Adverse Claims in District Court instead of a Proceeding Subsequent renders the judgment void. *Phillips v. Dolphin*, 776 N.W.2d 755 (Minn. App. 2009); Rule 215 Minn. Gen. R. Prac.

If the relief sought **incidentally** involves altering a Certificate of Title (example, probating the estate of a decedent who owned Torrens land, or dissolving the marriage of spouses who own Torrens land), the case is brought in the appropriate subject-matter court. The resulting decree must be approved by the Examiner of Titles before the Registrar can transfer title. Minn. Stat. 508.59 and 508.69

The crucial distinction is that a Court sitting in Proceedings Subsequent has statutory authority to direct the Registrar of Titles to alter the Certificate of Title under Minn. Stat. 508.71, but the Court sitting in Family, Housing, Probate or general District Court lacks personal jurisdiction over the Registrar of Titles.

The Order in a Family, Housing, Probate or general District Court case should not include language instructing the Registrar of Titles to do anything with Certificates of Title. The Registrar is obligated to disregard that language, causing confusion in the parties to the action and lowering the public's esteem for the judicial system.

We recommend **every divorce involving real estate include a Summary Real Estate Disposition Judgment** even though Minn. Stat. 518.191 says "may" and not "shall" because sooner or later, one of the parties will be required to record evidence of change in marital status.

VENUE: Minn. Stat. 542.02 provides actions relating to real estate shall be tried in the county where the real estate is located. Some causes of action have additional jurisdictional

Real Estate Reference Guide for Judges

requirements, set forth in the topic sections elsewhere in this guide.

Nathan Bissonette

Legal Descriptions

Summary	Not a separate cause of action, but a consideration in any action brought to alter the legal description of an owner's property
Statute	No specific statute. Arises in cases involving Adverse Possession, Practical Location, Registration of Boundaries, Reformation of a Document, Initial Registration and Proceedings Subsequent
Limitations	No specific statute; use statute of limitations for underlying cause of action
Necessary Parties	Everyone whose interests would be affected by the change: owners, easement holders, lenders whose collateral might be impaired, city or county road authority, State of Minnesota if lakeshore is involved
Elements Burden of Proof Standard of Proof Defenses	)) Varies with underlying cause of action))
Oddities	Both the abstract and Torrens systems of land records are organized by legal description. Using an incorrect or incomplete legal description in the Order makes it difficult to index against the correct legal description. What legal description should you use in your Order? **Best** source: a competent land surveyor;

Next best source: documents already recorded with the Recorder or shown on the Certificate of Title for Torrens land;

Reluctantly use the City of St. Paul's AMANDA system (variances, building permits); that's based on the property tax system's abbreviations so it's likely incomplete. If a better legal description was admitted into evidence, use that instead.

Avoid the property tax statement; that's an abbreviation for the convenience of the tax assessor, is generally not complete, and is not intended for drafting legal documents.

Special Torrens Note — If the relief sought is an alteration of the legal description shown on a Certificate of Title, the case must be brought as a Proceeding Subsequent under Minn. Stat. 508.71, Subd. 2. Rule 215 Minn. Gen. R. Prac. requires an order in a civil case that affects Torrens land to be approved as to form by Examiner of Titles before presentation to court.

Citations

In cases where the legal description itself is in dispute:
"It is a long-settled rule that when identifying boundary lines, fixed and known monuments or objects called for in a legal description prevail over given courses and distances; the order of application

being first, to natural objects; second, to artificial marks; and, third, to courses and distances."
>*Magnuson v. Cossette*, 707 N.W.2d 738, 744 (Minn. App. 2006)

A legal description is sufficient if the land so described can be located by a competent surveyor.
>*Daly v. Duwane Const. Co.*, 106 N.W.2d 631 (Minn. 1960)

Examples of insufficient legal descriptions are:
>Doesn't "close," meaning if you walk around the property following the legal description, you will not end up where you started.
>>*Application of Mrosak*, 415 N.W.2d 98 (Minn. App. 1987)

>Starts from a moving point like the shore of a lake, which changes with every wave and thereby moves the entire parcel back and forth.
>>*Application of Mrosak*, 415 N.W.2d 98 (Minn. App. 1987)

>Contains a call to an ambiguous point like "Charles Magnuson's place"
>>*Mattson Ridge, LLC v. Clear Rock Title, LLP*, 824 N.W.2d 622 (Minn. 2012)

An insufficient or defective legal description in a recorded instrument puts the public on notice that some interest is claimed and creates a duty in the buyer to further inquire as to that interest.
>*Howard, McRoberts & Murray v. Starry*, 382 N.W.2d 293 (Minn. App. 1986)

Standard of Proof is preponderance, when deciding which of competing legal descriptions best describe

Real Estate Reference Guide for Judges

the same land. Standard of Proof is clear and convincing when seeking to alter an existing legal description so that it covers different land – see **Reformation of a Document** section.

Life estate

Summary	Not a separate cause of action; a form of partial ownership
Statute	Minn. Stat. 500.01. Arises in cases involving Adverse Possession, Practical Location, Registration of Boundaries, Reformation of a Document, Initial Registration and Proceedings Subsequent
Limitations	No specific statute; use statute of limitations for underlying cause of action
Necessary Parties	Everyone whose interests would be affected by the change: owners, easement holders, lenders whose collateral might be impaired, city or county road authority, State of Minnesota if lakeshore is involved
Elements Burden of Proof Standard of Proof Defenses	)) Varies with underlying cause of action))
Oddities	Duration depends on the measuring life, often unstated. Usual: I give you a life estate, measured by your life. Possible: I give him a life estate, measured by your life (when you die, he moves out).
Special Torrens Note	If the relief sought is an alteration of the legal description shown on a Certificate of Title, the case must be brought as a Proceeding Subsequent under Minn. Stat. 508.71, Subd. 2. Rule 215 Minn. Gen. R. Prac. requires an

order in a civil case that affects Torrens land to be approved as to form by Examiner of Titles before presentation to court.

Citations

Owner Tessman gave a deed to friend Clark, reserving a life estate to Tessman, as an estate planning technique to defeat a medical assistance claim (note – this does NOT work, the attorney who advised them to do it was mistaken). Clark paid no consideration (indicative of a gift) but Tessman filed no gift tax return. When the parties had a falling out, the court determined the conveyance was not a valid gift because there was no donative intent and no clear evidence of acceptance of the deed. By long-established case-law, Clark as remainderman was responsible for paying the mortgage, which he did not, further evidence he did not consider the property to be his.

Tessman v. Clark, unpublished, A19-0791 (Minn. App. 2019).

2020 update: This section was new in 2020.

Marital Lien

Summary	Not a separate cause of action but a consideration in every divorce
Statute	Minn. Stat. 518.58; 541.03
Limitations	If given to secure the property division, or enforced as a mortgage, 15 years from date of maturity; all others, 10 years from date of maturity
Necessary Parties	Lien holder, land owner
Elements	Specific lien creation language Purpose of lien (what is secured by it) Method of enforcement
Burden of Proof	Lien holder
Standard of Proof	Preponderance
Defenses	Failure to create lien Expiration of lien
Oddities	Created and modified in Family Court. Enforced in Civil Court. Also known as "spousal lien," "equitable lien," homestead lien."
Special Torrens Note	A certified copy of a Judgment and Decree or Summary Real Estate Disposition Judgment can be recorded to show the dissolution of a marriage and creation of a marital lien, but title will not transfer and the lien will not appear on the Certificate of Title without a

deed from the divested spouse reserving the lien or a Certificate of Examiner noting the lien. The Summary Real Estate Disposition Judgment is STRONGLY encouraged.

If the relief sought is an alteration of the memorial of the marital lien shown in an instrument on a Certificate of Title, the case must be brought as a Proceeding Subsequent under Minn. Stat. 508.71, Subd. 2.

Rule 215 Minn. Gen. R. Prac. requires an order in a civil case that affects Torrens land to be approved as to form by Examiner of Titles before presentation to court.

Citations

If the marital lien is not given to secure the property division or if the decree does not state the lien will be enforced in the manner of a mortgage foreclosure by advertisement, then the marital lien must be reduced to judgment and enforced as a judgment lien (Writ of Execution under Chapter 550).

Drafting tip:
"Finally, to decrease the likelihood of such disputes, we suggest that courts using marital liens include in their orders: (1) the value of the debt to be secured by the lien, in terms of either an absolute dollar amount or a percentage of the equity or ultimate sale price of the property; (2) the applicable interest rate, if any, which should be justified in the accounting of the court's division of the marital assets, *see Thomas v. Thomas,* 407 N.W.2d 124, (Minn.App.1987) (requiring specific findings to explain decision not to require payment of interest); (3) an ascertainable date of maturity; (4) a specific mechanism for enforcement; and (5) an

explanation of whether the lien is in the nature of child support or purely a division of property, *see Holmberg v. Holmberg,* 578 N.W.2d 817, 825 & n. 8 (Minn.App.1998) (noting that lien in nature of child support is subject to modification, while divisions of property are final), *aff'd,* 588 N.W.2d 720 (Minn.1999)."
>Bakken V. Helgeson, 785 N.W.2d 791 (Minn. App. 2010)

See Title Standard 114 for additional cases and explanations.

2019 update: This section was new in 2019.

2023 update:

The court awarded the marital homestead to Husband subject to a lien in favor of Wife. Husband failed to satisfy the lien or pay the mortgage; the property went into foreclosure, the family court ordered the property sold; Husband refused to sign a purchase agreement and was found to be in constructive civil contempt which was upheld on appeal.

This case is cited for its futility. Rather than fighting with uncooperative parties (and possibly losing the equity in the home), we recommend the court appoint a Receiver with authority to conduct the sale and pay the money into court, to be divided by the court at a later hearing.
> *In re the Marriage of Lorbiecke v. Lorbiecke,* unpublished, A22-0943 (Minn. App. 2023).

Real Estate Reference Guide for Judges

Marital Rights

Summary	Not a separate cause of action but a consideration in every conveyance
Statute	Minn. Stat. 507.02, 507.03, 510.01
Limitations	)
Necessary Parties	)
Elements	) These vary with the underlying action.
Burden of Proof	)
Standard of Proof	)
Defenses	)

Oddities

Marital rights are not ownership, they're rights separate from ownership.

Marital rights arise at the instant of marriage and last until the marriage is terminated by divorce or death. A spouse might hold title to the land in her name alone, but her spouse still has marital rights.

Minn. Stat. 507.02 provides that no conveyance of the homestead is valid without the signature of all spouses. Minn. Stat. 507.03 provides exceptions only for: purchase-money mortgage a conveyance between spouses, or a severance of joint tenancy.

Special Torrens Note

A certified copy of a marriage certificate can be recorded on the Certificate of Title to show entry into a marriage, but title will not change without a deed adding the new spouse to title.

Nathan Bissonette

A certified copy of a Judgment and Decree, Certificate of Dissolution or Summary Real Estate Disposition Judgment can be recorded to show the dissolution of a marriage, but title will not transfer without a deed from the divested spouse or a Certificate of Examiner. Minn. Stat. 508.59. The Summary Real Estate Disposition Judgment is STRONGLY encouraged.

If the relief sought is an alteration of the marital status shown in an instrument on a Certificate of Title, the case must be brought as a Proceeding Subsequent under Minn. Stat. 508.71, Subd. 2.

Rule 215 Minn. Gen. R. Prac. requires an order in a civil case that affects Torrens land to be approved as to form by Examiner of Titles before presentation to court.

Citations
A conveyance that violates Minn. Stat. 507.02 is not merely voidable, it is void.
Dvorak v. Maring, 285 N.W.2d 675 (Minn. 1979)

"Homestead" for purposes of this statute is not determined by tax status, it is defined by Minn. Stat. 510.01 as the debtor's dwelling place. This raises a fact issue for a court to decide: was the property the dwelling place of one or both of the spouses on the date the conveyance was signed?
Marine Credit Union v. Detlefson-Delano, 830 N.W.2d 859 (Minn. 2013)

A mortgage is a conveyance subject to Minn. Stat. 507.02.
National City Bank v. Engler, 777 N.W.2d 762 (Minn. App. 2010)

Real Estate Reference Guide for Judges

"Spouse" for purposes of giving a mortgage includes legally married spouses and also putative spouses under Minn. Stat. 518.055.
> *Rahma Nur-Afi v. Guidance Residential, LLC,* Civil Case No. 08-5096 (DWF/SRN) (D. Minn. 2010), order entered September 7, 2010 by Judge Frank
> *Choa Yang Xiong v. Su Xiong,* 800 N.W.2d 187 (Minn. App. 2011)

If putative spouse status is claimed, make detailed findings for or against.
> *Yang v. Fang,* A14-1158 unpublished (Minn. App. 2015)

A conveyance (including a mortgage) not signed by one of the spouses is facially void but lenders may seek equitable relief. Where the non-signing spouse knew about the mortgage and received the money from the loan it secured, she was estopped from asserting her non-signature as a defense to enforcement of the mortgage.
> *Karnitz v. Wells Fargo Bank, N.A.,* 572 F.3d 572 (8th Cir., 2009)

2018 update:
Rights of putative spouses discussed. Note the dissenting opinion.
> *Fonoti v. Fonoti,* unpublished, A17-0091 (Minn. App. 2018)

Marketable Title Act (40-year law)

Summary	Obsolete rights shouldn't burden land forever. By statute, some become unenforceable after a time. This statute is a defense to enforcement.
Statute	Minn. Stat. 541.023
Limitation	40 years since last recorded renewal
Necessary Parties	Land owner, holder of rights claimed to be unenforceable, persons affected by the action
Elements	This is not a cause of action, it is a defense to a cause of action
Burden of Proof	Plaintiff
Standard of Proof	Preponderance
Defenses	Rights sought to be limited does not fall under this statute (but see Marketable Title Act: 30-year law); 40-year period has not elapsed
Oddities	Cannot use to cut off rights of federal government, railroads, public service corporations, schools, churches, or persons in possession.
Special Torrens Note	Does not apply to Torrens land; Minn. Stat. 541.023, Subd. 2, was enacted to overturn the holding in *Hersh Properties, LLC v. McDonald's Corporation,* 588 N.W.2d 728 (Minn. 1999) in which the Court determined that it applied to Torrens land.

Real Estate Reference Guide for Judges

Citations
> "Ancient records shall not fetter the marketability of real estate"
> *Wichelman v. Messner*, 83 N.W.2d 800 (Minn. 1957). Interplay between 40-year law and 30-year law explained.

Marketable Title Act does not cut off persons in possession of an easement, even if more than 40 years old and no renewal recorded.
> *In Re Sampair v. Village of Birchwood*, 784 N.W.2d 65 (Minn. 2010)

The Marketable Title Act does not act offensively to provide foundation for new title, but defensively to protect preexisting claims of title.
> *Padrnos v. City of Nisswa,* 409 N.W.2d 36 (Minn. App. 1987)

2019 update:
Road was created by County Board Order in 1869, never recorded with the county land records. Even though not recorded, once created, the road is not subject to the Marketable Title Act (no need to continuously record renewal notices) because the existence of the road is sufficient notice of the public's rights.
> *County of Pope v. Kirkeby,* A18-0406, unpublished (Minn. App. 2018)

2022 update:
The Minnesota Marketable Title Act applies to land dedicated by plat to public use and extinguishes any public interest in such land that is not properly recorded under the act. REVERSED SEE BELOW

> *In re Moratzka*, unpublished, A21-0829, A21-0832 (Minn. App. 2022)

A deed that conveys a fee simple interest in part of a platted street along with a conveyance of the abutting lot is a "source of title" to that part of the street for purposes of the Marketable Title Act. Since the Marketable Title Act applies to platted streets under *Moratzka*, the land now belongs to Plaintiff. PROBABLY OVERRULED SEE BELOW.

> *Lundstrom v. Township of Florence*, unpublished, A21-1714 (Minn. App. 2022)

2023 Update:

Supreme Court reversed the Court of Appeals opinion in Moratzka, above. The Marketable Title Act does not apply to land dedicated to public use by plat. A street platted 100 years ago but still undeveloped for public use is not extinguished by the 40-year law.
> *In re Moratzka,* [citation pending] A21-0829, A21-0832 March 29, 2023 (Minn. 2023)

Though not expressly stated in the opinion, the Lundstrom case cited in the 2022 update is probably over-ruled because it relied on the same erroneous construction of the Marketable Title Act.

Real Estate Reference Guide for Judges

Mechanic's Lien

Summary	Action to declare a lien on land and to satisfy the lien by selling the land
Statute	Minn. Stat. Chapter 514
Limitation	Must perfect lien within 120 days of last item claimed. Minn. Stat. 514.08 Lien becomes unenforceable one year after date of last item claimed if action not commenced by then. Minn. Stat. 514.12, Subd. 3.
Necessary Parties	Landowner of record, lien holders, occupants, other mechanic's lien claimants.
Elements	Labor, skill, materials, services (see list Minn. Stat. 514.01) that improved real estate. Must prove legal description of land improved and value of improvement.
Burden of Proof	Person claiming the lien
Standard of Proof	Preponderance
Defenses procedure:	Most common defenses are errors in<ul><li>Failure to timely give pre-lien notice when required</li><li>Failure to timely serve and file Mechanic's Lien Statement</li><li>Recording lien statement in the wrong office or in the wrong county</li><li>Failure to describe the affected property with reasonable certainty</li><li>Overstating the amount of the lien</li></ul>

Version 7.1   July 1, 2023

	Failure to timely commence the action to enforce the lien, to file the Lis Pendens, to file the pleadings or to serve necessary parties Unlicensed claimant (Minn. Stat. 326B.845) Waiver of lien rights
Oddities	Service and filing is backwards (like an eviction): the Complaint is filed in the Court File BEFORE the Summons is served. Minn. Stat. 514.11. It's jurisdictional – failure is fatal. Answer must be filed within 20 days of service of the Complaint.
	The Rules of Civil Procedure do not govern mechanic's lien actions where the Rules conflict with the lien statute. Minn. R. Civ. P. 81.01(a) and Appendix A.
Special Torrens Note	Mechanic's liens use a unique statutory process; they are not brought as Proceedings Subsequent under Minn. Stat. 508.71, Subd. 2.
	Rule 215 Minn. Gen. R. Prac., which requires an order in a civil case that affects Torrens land to be approved as to form by Examiner of Titles before presentation to court, does **not** apply to these actions.

Citations
    <u>Formation and Attachment of Lien</u>
        Contractors and sub-contractors must warn the landowner of their right to file a mechanic's lien by giving pre-lien notice. Specific requirements for timing, wording, service and exceptions are provided in Minn. Stat. 514.011.

A mechanic's lien claimant perfects a mechanic's lien by serving and filing a Mechanic's Lien Statement. Specific requirements for timing, wording and service are provided in Minn. Stat. 514.08.

A mechanic's lien must be reduced to civil judgment before it can be enforced. Specific requirements for timing, service, venue, Lis Pendens and pleadings are provided in Minn. Stat. 514.10.

A mechanic's lien is strictly construed as to whether a lien attaches but is liberally construed after the lien has been created.
    Dolder v. Griffin, 323 N.W.2d 773 (Minn. 1982)

Procedure to Enforce Lien

There is no right to a jury trial in a mechanic's lien action.
    Johnson Service Co. v. Kruse, 140 N.W. 118 (Minn. 1913)

The burden of proof is on the mechanic's lien claimant. The standard of proof is preponderance.
    Lundell v. Ahlman, 54 N.W. 936 (Minn. 1893); *Rich Johnson Homes, Inc., v. Sheehan,* A07-758 unpublished (Minn. App. 2008)

A prevailing claimant is entitled to "costs and disbursements" pursuant to Minn. Stat. 514.14, includes reasonable attorney's fees. The amount of attorney's fees is discretionary and need not be proportionate to overall recovery.
    Jadwin v. Kasal, 318 N.W.2d 844 (Minn. 1982)

Some judges construe the language of Minn. Stat. 514.10 regarding the amount of the bond to release a mechanic's lien before trial as limiting plaintiff's attorney's fees to double the amounts provided for foreclosure of a mortgage as set forth in Minn. Stat. 582.01. **This is a misreading of the statute.** Minn. Stat. 582.01, Subd. 1a limits fees in Foreclosure by Advertisement because that's a relatively simple statutory procedure. Minn. Stat. 582.01 Subd. 2 provides the court shall determine the award of attorney's fees in a Foreclosure by Action because litigation consumes more attorney time. The same analysis is true in a Mechanic's Lien Foreclosure action.

Defenses

Failure to perfect lien (pre-lien notice, untimely) is defense.
> *Dolder v. Griffin*, 323 N.W.2d 773 (Minn. 1982)

If the claimant has knowingly demanded more in the mechanic's lien statement than is justly due, the claimant loses its lien; requires a showing of fraud, bad faith or intentional excess demand.
> Minn. Stat. 514.74. *R. B. Thompson, Jr. Lumber Co. v. Windsor Development Corp.*, 383 N.W.2d 357 (Minn. App. 1986)

The common law "constitutional lien" is entirely different, it arises from Article 1, Section 12 of the Minnesota Constitution.
> *ServiceMaster of St. Cloud v. GAB Business Services, Inc.*, 544 N.W.2d 302 (Minn. 1996)

Homesteads are not exempt from mechanic's liens, but public property may be.

Minn. Stat. 510.01. *Comstock & Davis, Inc., v. City of Eden Prairie,* 557 N.W.2d 213 (Minn. App. 1997)

Priority

Mechanic's liens "relate back" to the first visible sign of improvements, meaning they have priority over later-recorded encumbrances such as mortgages. Minn. Stat. 514.05.

Reuben E. Johnson Co. v. Phelps, 156 N.W.2d 247 (Minn. 1968)

For purposes of determining priority over other liens, mechanic's liens relate back to the first visible sign of improvement, and all mechanic's liens have the same relate-back date, regardless of when their specific work was done.

Minn. Stat. 514.05; *Big Lake Lumber, Inc., v. Security Property Investments, Inc.,* 820 N.W.2d 253 (Minn. App. 2012)

As between themselves, all mechanics' liens share the same priority date.

Minn. Stat. 514.05 and 514.15. *Miller v. Stoddard,* 56 N.W. 131 (Minn. 1893)

Actual notice can alter priority. A mechanic's lien claimant that has actual notice of an unrecorded mortgage before the lien claimant starts work, can be subordinated to the unrecorded mortgage. Minn. Stat. 514.05. *Rudd Lumber Co. v. Anderson,* 201 N.W. 548 (Minn. 1925), but see *Mavco, Inc. v. Eggink,* 739 N.W.2d 148 (Minn. 2007) holding that the holder of a later-recorded mortgage was not a necessary party so failure to name it did not affect priority.

A mortgage lender that has actual notice of an unrecorded mechanic's lien before the lender records its mortgage, can be subordinated to the unrecorded mechanic's lien.
> Minn. Stat. 514.05. *Riverview Muir Doran, LLC v. JADT Development Group, LLC*, 790 N.W.2d 167 (Minn. 2010)

Judgment should state:
> The amount of the lien. A mechanic's lien claimant is entitled to judgment under Minn. Stat. 514.03:
>> If there was a contract, for the contract amount; or
>> If there was no contract, for the reasonable value of the work done and the skill, material and machinery furnished, including a reasonable profit.
>> *Enviro-Fab, Inc., v. Blandin Paper Company*, 349 N.W.2d 842 (Minn. App. 1984)
>
> The legal description of lands subject to the lien. If the claimant has contributed to the improvement of several contiguous parcels (example, several lots in a residential subdivision), the lien claimant may claim a blanket lien against all those lots or separate liens against individual lots. Minn. Stat. 514.09
>
> The priority of the lien, as against other encumbrances (see below).
>
> The amount of pre-judgment interest to be added to the lien.
>> If there is a written agreement, the contract rate controls.

Real Estate Reference Guide for Judges

McCarron's Building Center v. Titus Construction, Inc., A09-1571, unpublished (Minn. App. 2010)

If there is no written agreement, the statutory interest rate under Minn. Stat. 334.01 controls. Minn. Stat. 514.135.
John David Contracting, Inc., v. Brozek, 535 N.W.2d 397 (Minn. App. 1995)

Attorney's Fees. A prevailing claimant may recover attorney's fees.
Jadwin v. Kasal, 318 N.W.2d 844 (Minn. 1982)

Order to Sell. The Judgment must order the Sheriff to sell the lands encumbered by the lien. Minn. Stat. 514.15.

Redemption period. The period of time the foreclosed owner has to redeem from the sale of the property.

Sale

The judgment directs the sale of the property and the manner of the sale (Minn. Stat. 514.15) provided, however, that redemption rights must be as set forth in Minn. Stat. 550.24.

Generally, the sale is conducted in the same manner as sales on an execution of judgment under Minn. Stat. 550.04. The procedures are detailed but scattered throughout the statutes. If the sale procedures are the contested issue, a host of CLE publications provide excellent guidance.

Redemption. The owner may redeem from the Sheriff's Sale. The length of the redemption period is determined by statute. If the owner fails to redeem, junior lien holders may redeem in order of priority. Upon receiving payment in redemption, the Sheriff will issue a Certificate of Redemption which must be recorded with the Registrar/Recorder. Minn. Stat. 514.15, 550.24

2018 update:
Contractor substantially performed most of the contract, homeowner is entitled to offsets for work not performed, attorney's fees of six times the judgment award upheld.
Sela Roofing and Remodeling, Inc., v. Moot, unpublished, A16-1862 (Minn. App. 2017)

2019 update:
Co-owner who redeems the whole property from foreclosure, has a pledge or mortgage against the other owner's interest for that share of the redemption, and this was superior to an existing junior mortgage. The redemptor does not take ownership of the whole.
Buettel v. Harmount, 46 Minn. 481 (1891)

2021 update:
Invoices and testimony as to labor and materials provided established the reasonable value of improvements. Mechanic's lien claimants are entitled to attorneys' fees by statute but must bring a motion under Rule 119 Gen. R. Prac. supported by documentation so the court can hold a hearing on the amount of fees to be awarded. In the absence of a written agreement, the maximum rate of interest is 6% as provided under Minn. Stat. 334.01.
Brothers Fire Protection Co. v. Przymus, unpublished, A20-0920 (Minn. App. 2021)

Real Estate Reference Guide for Judges

Removing $50,000 of fallen trees after a severe storm was not an "improvement to property" and therefore the claimant was not entitled to a mechanic's lien.
> *Koppi v. Marsh*, unpublished, A19-1492 (Minn. App. 2020)

Minn. Stat. 514.14 entitles the mechanic's lien claimant to costs and disbursements, which includes attorney's fees, *Jadwin v. Kasal*, 318 N. W. 2d 844 (Minn. 1982), the amount of which must be reasonable based on the nine Jadwin factors and must be in reasonable relation to the amount of the judgment secured. *Northwest Wholesale Lumber, Inc., v. Citadel Co.* 457 N.W.2d 244 (Minn. App. 1990). The request for fees of $39,976 was reduced down to $5,000 because: "As outlined in the factors, this case was overworked and overbilled by six attorneys, three law clerks, and three paralegals especially in light of the amount in controversy and complexity of the issues."
> *ProStar Exteriors, LLC v. Walker*, unpublished, A20-0862 (Minn. App. 2021)

2022 update:

Prelien notice and Lis Pendens requirements discussed. "Paid in full" language on a check to the general contractor does not automatically preclude a mechanic's lien by a subcontractor.
> *ALL, Inc. v. Hagen*, unpublished, A21-0459 (Minn. App. 2021)

Not a mechanic's lien case - a breach of contract case - but another check marked "paid in full," a frequent topic in mechanic's lien disputes.
> *Detailed by Design LLC v. Langer*, unpublished, A21-0879 (Minn. App. 2022)

Contractor who failed to file a Mechanic's Lien cannot later assert a claim for unjust enrichment.
Scherber v. Bullock, unpublished, A21-0428 (Minn. App. 2022)

2023 update:

One lawyer represented two claimants (Day and Accredited) but failed to separate his billing between the two clients. On judgment for Accredited, the district court reduced his attorney's fees so that fees expended representing Day were not shifted onto Accredited's fee claim. Citing the trial court's analysis of the *Jadwin* factors, the appellate court held an award of $17,165 in fees on a claim of $3,719.56 was not unreasonable merely because the fees exceeded the amount of the lien. "Limiting fees in such a matter would discourage small lienholders from pursuing valid claims through the legal system," quoting *Kirkwold Construction Co. v. M.G.A. Construction Inc.*, 498 N.W.2d 465, 470 (Minn. App. 1993).
Accredited Electrical Solutions. v. PinPoint Homes, LLC, unpublished, A22-1059 (Minn. App. 2023)

A labor union can file a mechanic's lien to recover the value of fringe benefits owed to its members. "TCPT is a proper lien claimant because it is acting as the representative of the employees who performed labor that contributed to the improvement of real estate."
Twin City Pipe Trades Service Association, Inc., v. Peak Mechanical, Inc. 689 N.W. 2d 549 (Minn. App. 2004)

Although Twin City Pipe Trades mandates a strict construction of the mechanic's lien statute, the inquiry in that case was whether the trustee of an employment-benefit fund was a proper mechanic's lien claimant. The case does not hold that minor omissions in a mechanic's lien statement render it invalid.
NewMech Companies, Inc., v. Grove Hospitality, LLC, unpublished, A11-1346 (Minn. App. 2012)

Real Estate Reference Guide for Judges

As there is no right to a jury trial in a mechanic's lien foreclosure case, there is no right to a jury trial on any counterclaim brought in response to the foreclosure. Where the construction contract requires modifications to be in writing but the parties' course of performance demonstrates that the owner tends to direct changes to the construction contract orally, those directions constitute a waiver of the requirement that modifications be in writing.
R. J. Marco Construction, Inc. v. SAMS Enterprises, unpublished, A04-1433 (Minn. App. 2005)

Name

The Abstract and Torrens systems both maintain a Tract Index which is arranged by legal description. But, they also maintain second index, a Grantor-Grantee Index, which is arranged alphabetically. Using an incorrect or incomplete name makes it difficult to index the Order against the correct chain of title. **Exact spelling matters!**

The name "Sarah Smith Jones" is filed under "J" for Jones; but "Sarah Smith-Jones" is filed under "S" for Smith. **Hyphens matter!**

The Order should use the TRUE official, government-issued names, not aka, fka, or aliases.

Source document examples:

Birth Certificate	Minnesota Rules 4601.2525
Marriage Certificate	Minn. Stat. 517.10
Divorce Decree	Minn. Stat. 518.27
Court Ordered change	Minn. Stat. 259.11
Adoption Decree	Minn. Stat. 259.57
Naturalization Certificate	8 CFR 338.2
Articles of Incorporation	Minn. Stat. 302A.111
Articles of Organization of LLC	Minn. Stat. 322B.115

Most forms of personal ID are hearsay because they rely on one of the above. Do not accept hearsay evidence if source evidence is available. Be wary of Driver's License and Passport; they often are issued in the name used in the application form, not the Applicant's True Name.

Exception: if a party has used different names in the past, make these Findings: state all prior names used, find that they all refer to the same person, and make a Finding of the person's True Name. This will help the Registrar/Recorder link the Order to the party's name in the land records. List the True Name first, then list fka's and aliases.

Special Torrens Note:

If the land is Torrens, the Court should use the names shown on the Certificate of Title. If those names must be changed, the Examiner of Titles should be consulted. It may be the Certificate is wrong, or it may be a Name Directive should be issued under Minn. Stat. 508.71, Subd. 3. Rule 215 Minn. Gen. R. Prac. requires an order in civil case that affects Torrens land to be approved as to form by Examiner of Titles before presentation to court.

Option, Right of First Refusal, Right of First Offer

Summary The contractual right to buy land in the future. These are not present rights in real estate; the holder has no "title;" the rights derive from the contract, are analyzed under contract law and are enforced as contracts.

Keyword concepts:

Option – Set Terms. Seller and Buyer agree that Buyer can purchase on the set terms, if Buyer chooses to.

First Refusal – Intercept Sale. Buyer steps into the shoes of another potential buyer in a pending sale.

First Offer – Demand Purchase. Seller forces Buyer to put up or shut up.

Statute Minn. Stat. 513.05 (Statute of Frauds)

Limitations Minn. Stat. 501A.01(a) Rule Against Perpetuities

Necessary Parties Parties to agreement; owner of land; intercepted buyer

Elements Varies by theory

Burden of Proof Person seeking relief (enforcement or termination)

Real Estate Reference Guide for Judges

Standard of Proof	Preponderance
Defenses	Varies by theory
Oddities	Minn. Stat. 500.245, Right of First Refusal for Ag Land

If the court finds in favor of the person claiming they bought the land under one of these claims but a deed wasn't given, the court may order the seller to issue a deed. In that situation, the order also should provide that if the seller fails to do so, recording a certified copy of the court's order will have the effect of a conveyance to the buyer under Rule 70 Minn. R. Civ. Pro, divesting title from the seller and vesting it in buyer.

Special Torrens Note

If the relief primarily sought is enforcement of the contract right and not a change to the Certificate of Title, these cases need not be brought as Proceedings Subsequent, but Rule 215 Minn. Gen. R. Prac. requires an order in a civil case that affects Torrens land to be approved as to form by Examiner of Titles before presentation to court.

If the relief primarily sought is to alter a Certificate of Title, the case must be brought as a Proceeding Subsequent.

Citations

Option

An option agreement is a unilateral contract. It is not covered by the requirement of Minn. Stat. 513.01 that it be capable of being performed within one year.

Shaughnessy v. Eidsmo, 23 N.W.2d 362 (1946)

An option is generally outside the statute of frauds requirement that a conveyance of land be in writing because an option conveys no interest in land. An option is subject to Minn. Stat. 513.05 when relied upon as a memorandum of a contract for the sale of real estate.
> *Malevich v. Hakola*, 278 N.W.2d 541 (Minn. 1979)

Although an oral contract with an oral option to buy real estate and subsequent part performance was upheld in *Shaughnessy v. Eidsmo*, 23 N.W.2d 362 (1946), the Supreme Court has cautioned that options should be reduced to writing. Oral statements cannot be relied upon to establish the written contract of sale.
> *Olympik Village Apartments Limited Partnership vs. Rochester Lodge No. 13*, 2000 WL 782012, C7-99-1983 unpublished (Minn. App. 2000)

Where Landlord granted Tenant "a first option to extend this lease for an additional five (5) years, the terms and conditions *to be agreed upon at the time of the option renewal*"; Court held that provision (and similar "first option to purchase") to be unenforceable. The terms of the option, like any other contract, must be definite and certain.
> *King v. Dalton Motors Inc.*, 109 N.W.2d 51 (1961)

Right of First Refusal

A right of first refusal is a contract that gives the holder a contractual right to meet the terms of a third party offer. A right of first refusal does not convey

title, it ripens into an option to purchase the property. It is an *in personum* right.
> *Hempel v. Creek House Trust,* A08-1288, unpublished (Minn. App. 2009) quoting its earlier holding in *Hempel v. Creek House Trust,* 743 N.W.2d 305 (Minn. App. 2007)

The buyer failed to exercise his right of first refusal (good explanation of how it works)
> *Electric Fetus Company, Inc. v. Gonyea,* C1-00-545 unpublished (Minn. App. 2000)

Right of First Refusal of Ag Land

Farmers have special protection. The statute is detailed and specific. Unless a corporate owner of ag land complies with Minn. Stat. 500.245, it cannot contract to lease or sell ag land.
> *Gesell Concrete Products., Inc., v. Anderson,* A06-513, unpublished (Minn. App. 2007)
> *Ag Services of America, Inc., v. Schroeder,* 693 N.W.2d 227 (Minn. App. 2005)

Right of First Offer

This is conceptually different from a Right of First Refusal, but the courts seem to mix them up in the cases.

A Right of First Offer says "If you decide to sell, you must come to me first and tell me what terms you'd find acceptable, so I can decide whether to make an offer on those terms; and if I do, you're required to accept my offer."

A Right of First Refusal says "If you sign a purchase agreement to sell to someone else, I can choose to match the terms of that agreement and if I do, I step into the shoes of the other buyer and you're required to sell to me on those terms."

I found only two cases on First Offers and they have convoluted facts with little explanation:

Owner sold land to Buyer and gave a Right of First Offer on the remaining land, then signed a purchase agreement to sell it to someone else subject to Buyer's right. When the sale fell through, the agent who arranged the sale sued for tortious interference with contract and the buyer sued to compel Owner to convey pursuant to Buyer's Right of First Offer.
Lehn v. Kolles, A03-1602 unpublished (Minn. App. 2004)

Sprint (the cell phone company) held the FCC license to operate on certain radio frequencies in the Saginaw, Michigan area. Sprint licensed Speednet to use Sprint's frequencies. The license agreement contained a Right of First Offer requiring Speednet to offer to sell its assets to Sprint before selling to any other entity. Speednet negotiated a sale to Clearwire instead. Sprint sought an injunction to block the sale. The case isn't about real estate but has a nice explanation.
PCTV Gold, Inc., v. Speednet, LLC, 508 F.3d 1137 (8th Cir., 2007)

2018 update:

Options, Rights of First Refusal and Rights of First Offer were covered by Thomas Hauschild and John Wheaton at the 2017 Real Estate Institute, materials available from Minnesota CLE.

2020 update:

Real Estate Reference Guide for Judges

A settlement agreement that included a 90-day option to purchase did not commence until the option was recorded. Notice to exercise the option before the agreement was recorded did not trigger the 90-day period to exercise the option.
Goerdt v. Goerdt, unpublished, A18-1847 (Minn. App. 2019).

2023 update:

Buyer held a right of first refusal to purchase 47 acres from Seller, except the portion of such lands as Seller conveyed to his children. Seller executed a TODD to his daughters for the whole 47 acres, then died. Daughters signed a purchase agreement to Third Party, subject to cancellation of Buyer's right of first refusal and also signed a purchase agreement to Buyer, subject to cancellation of Third Party's purchase agreement. Held: a first right of refusal is a contract right, not an interest in real property. It does not run with the land to impose obligations on successor owners. Buyer's first right of refusal was terminated by the TODD transfer to Seller's children.
Braith v. Duban, unpublished, A21-1554 (Minn. App. 2022)

Kevin held an option to buy the family farm from his mother, Evelyn, for $200,000. Four decades later, Kevin sent Evelyn a letter saying he already paid the purchase price in full, mostly by his labor, and asking for a deed. Held: sending a letter did not exercise Kevin's option and therefore did not require Evelyn to convey.
Bruntlett v. Bruntlett, A22-0331 unpublished (Minn. App. 2023)

Partition

Summary	When owners can't agree, the court divides the land or orders it sold and divides the proceeds of sale.
Statute	Minn. Stat. Chapter 558
Limitations	None
Necessary Parties	Owners and known lien holders. May also serve "all other persons unknown having or claiming an interest in the property described in the complaint herein," but see rights of tenants under Minn. Stat. 558.08.
Elements	Plaintiff has an interest in real estate owned with others, but not all agree.
Burden of Proof	Once Plaintiff establishes a right to seek partition, the court determines the result using its general equitable powers within the statutory framework.
Standard of Proof	None
Defenses	Not a person entitled to seek partition Failure to timely record Notice of Lis Pendens
Oddities	Court determines rights of parties, then appoints three "disinterested and judicious citizens" as referees to recommend method of partition (land or money) for court approval. Minn. Stat. 558.04 If dividing the land would cause great prejudice to the owners, court may order

property sold. Minn. Stat. 558.14. Often a problem in urban areas where subdividing a lot would violate zoning laws.

Action for partition is different from "partition fence" as defined in Minn. Stat. 344.01-20.

If the court awards title to one party, the court may order the other parties to issue a deed upon payment of money. In that situation, the order also should provide that if the seller fails to do so, recording a certified copy of the court's order will have the effect of a conveyance to the buyer under Rule 70 Minn. R. Civ. Pro, divesting title from the seller and vesting it in buyer.

Special Torrens Note   Not brought as Proceeding Subsequent, even if land is Torrens. Rule 215 Minn. Gen. R. Prac. requires an order in a civil case that affects Torrens land to be approved as to form by Examiner of Titles before presentation to court.

Citations

Parties must be co-tenants. *Swanson v. Swanson,* 856 N.W.2d 705 (Minn. App. 2014)

Best description of partition history is *Swogger v. Taylor*, 68 N.W.2d 376 (Minn. 1955)

2020 update:

District Court erred by setting aside and failing to confirm partition referees' report. Reversed.
Neumann v. Anderson, 916 N.W.2d 41 (Minn. App. 2018)

Unmarried property owners separated and agreed to sell the house and divide proceeds in Partition action. Court's findings on respective contributions were not clearly erroneous, appeals court defers to trial court on issues of credibility, no showing of prejudice from certain acts, no abuse of discretion in crediting certain payments.

Henel v. Salas, unpublished, A19-0431, (Minn. App. 2020).

2021 update:

The award of reasonable attorney's fees in a partition action pursuant to Minn. Stat. 558.10 does not violate the separation of powers doctrine and is proper where the final partition order benefits all parties. In this case, all parties benefitted from the partition sale because it resolved their contentious, untenable joint ownership of the property.

Campbell v. Larson, unpublished, A20-1068 (Minn. App. 2021)

2023 update:

Referees partition the property in accordance with the court's judgment. The referees do not decide the rights of the parties. The requirement for a pre-sale appraisal applies to private sales, not public sales.

Simmons v. Mason, unpublished, A22-0435 (Minn. App. 2023)

Practical Location

Summary	An action to adjust boundary lines to conform to actual use (example, fence not on platted lot line but used as the boundary).
Statute	None, usually pled as declaratory judgment under Chapter 555. Could arise in Initial Registration, Proceeding Subsequent or Action to Determine Boundaries under Minn. Stat. 508.671 or 559.23
Limitations	None, Minn. Stat. 541.02 does not apply.
Necessary Parties	Landowner of record, lien holders, occupants and encroachers, other persons known to Plaintiff to claim an interest that does not appear of record
Elements	Varies by legal theory, equitable action:

To establish a boundary by practical location through **acquiescence**, "a person must show by evidence that is clear, positive, and unequivocal that the alleged property line was acquiesced in for a sufficient length of time to bar a right of entry under the statute of limitations," which is 15 years in Minnesota. The acquiescence required is not merely passive consent but conduct from which assent may be reasonably inferred.

To establish a boundary by practical location through **express agreement**, a person must prove that an express agreement between the landowners sets an 'exact, precise line' between their properties and that the agreement had been acquiesced in 'for a considerable time.'

To establish a boundary by **estoppel**, the party whose rights are to be barred must have silently looked on with knowledge of the true line while the other party encroached thereon or subjected himself to expense which he would not have incurred had the line been in dispute.

Defenses	Failure to prove all elements of theory pled
Burden of Proof	Person asserting the new boundary line
Standard of Proof	The evidence of the new boundary line must be clear, positive and unequivocal. The new boundary line must be certain, visible and well-known.
Oddities	While not specifically required by any case, your Examiner cannot conceive of a "certain, visible and well-known line" that isn't marked by some specific object the landowners could see to use as the basis for the boundary line, such as a fence or row of trees. The final Order should include a finding of the object and evidence that established the line. **Good practice to require a survey and have the surveyor write the legal description of the boundary line.**
Special	

Real Estate Reference Guide for Judges

Torrens Note

If the land is Torrens and the relief sought is to change the legal description shown on the Certificate of Title, the action must be brought as a Proceeding Subsequent.

Rule 215 Minn. Gen. R. Prac. requires an order in a civil case that affects Torrens land to be approved as to form by Examiner of Titles before presentation to court.

Citations

A boundary clearly and convincingly established by practical location may prevail over the contrary result of a survey.
Phillips v. Blowers, 161 N.W.2d 524 (Minn. 1968)

Three theories to prove a new boundary line by Practical Location:

1) Acquiescence: The location relied upon must have been acquiesced in for a sufficient length of time to bar a right of entry under the statute of limitations;

   To establish a boundary by practical location through acquiescence, "a person must show by evidence that is clear, positive, and unequivocal that the alleged property line was acquiesced in for a sufficient length of time to bar a right of entry under the statute of limitations," which is 15 years in Minnesota. The acquiescence required is not merely passive consent but conduct from which assent may be reasonably inferred.
   Britney v. Swan Lake Cabin Corp., 795 N.W.2d 867 (Minn. App. 2011)

2) Agreement: The line must have been expressly agreed upon by the interested parties and afterwards acquiesced in;

To establish a boundary by practical location through express agreement, a person must prove that an express agreement between the landowners set an 'exact, precise line' between their properties and that the agreement had been acquiesced to 'for a considerable time.'
Beardsley v. Crane, 54 N.W. 740 (Minn. 1893)

Without a specific discussion identifying the boundary line or a specific boundary-related action clearly proving that the parties or their predecessors in interest had agreed to a specific boundary, a boundary is not established by practical location based on express agreement . . . An express agreement requires more than unilaterally assumed, unspoken and unwritten mutual agreements corroborated by neither word nor act.
Slindee v. Fritch Investments, LLC, 760 N.W.2d 903 (Minn. App. 2009)

3) Estoppel: The party whose rights are to be barred must have silently looked on with knowledge of the true line while the other party encroached thereon or subjected himself to expense which he would not have incurred had the line been in dispute.

Estoppel requires knowing silence on the part of the party to be charged and unknowing detriment by the other.
Theros v. Phillips, 256 N.W.2d 852 at 859 (Minn. 1977)

Real Estate Reference Guide for Judges

Boundary by Practical Location awards fee title, not easement or license.
    Gabler v. Fedoruk, 756 N.W.2d 725 (Minn. App. 2008)

The burden of proof is on the person asserting the new boundary line.
    Bjerketvedt v. Jacobson, 44 N.W.2d 775 (Minn. 1950)

The standard of proof is: the evidence of the new boundary line must be clear, positive and unequivocal.
    Britney v. Swan Lake Cabin Corp., 795 N.W.2d 867 (Minn. App. 2011)

The new boundary line must be certain, visible and well-known.
    Beardsley v. Crane, 54 N.W. 740 (Minn. 1893)

Necessary parties include anybody whose rights in the disputed lands would be affected by the action, including owners shown in the property records, occupants who may hold under an unrecorded deed, the holder of an easement over the disputed land and a lender whose loan is secured by a mortgage on the disputed land. Persons whose rights are affected but who were not made parties are not bound by the Order. For judicial economy, consider ordering the Plaintiff to produce an Owner's and Encumbrancer's Report to find all necessary parties and thereby avoid repeat litigation.

Laches is not a defense to boundary by practical location.
    In re Cummins, A14-0737, unpublished (Minn. App. 2015)

Order should include:

Findings of Fact reciting the evidence for each factor and sub-factor of the particular theory advanced by Plaintiff and legal descriptions of the affected properties and of the new boundary line.

Conclusion of Law stating evidence was clear, positive and unequivocal

Legal description of the boundary as determined by the Court

What's the Thing? Mention the Thing in the Order.
While not specifically required by any case, Your Examiner cannot conceive of a "certain, visible and well-known line" that isn't marked by a particular Thing that the landowners could see to use as the basis for the boundary line.

Examples:
Dike
Del Schnabel v. Rask, A11-2237 unpublished (Minn. App. 2012)

Fence
Wojahn v. Johnson, 297 N.W.2d 298 (Minn. 1980)
Fredrickson v. Riepe, A11-158 unpublished (Minn. App. 2011)

Gravel road, garage and cement slab
Watkins v. Patch, A12-2119 unpublished (Minn. App. 2013)

Lines of trees
Phillips v. Blowers, 161 N.W.2d 524 (Minn. 1968)

Pipeline

Real Estate Reference Guide for Judges

Enbridge Energy, LP v. Dyrdal, A11-381 unpublished (Minn. App. 2011)

String line for road
Erickson v. Symiczek, A12-1821 unpublished (Minn. App. 2013)

Things the courts have said were NOT sufficient to establish boundary by practical location:

Row of painted rocks
Gifford v. Vore, 72 N.W.2d 625 (Minn. 1955)

Survey of heavily wooded area and raising sheep on disputed lands
Pratt Investment Company v. Kennedy, 636 N.W.2d 844 (Minn. App. 2001)

Partly contrary to the author's opinion, the Court of Appeals has held:
> Respondents argue that the district court should have held that appellants were also required to present evidence of an established visible boundary line to succeed in their claim for boundary by estoppel. However, no case-law is cited holding that a visible boundary line is required in a claim for boundary by estoppel.
> *Petition of Jacobsen,* A13-0758 unpublished (Minn. App. 2013)

2018 update:

The "clear-error" standard of review applies even when the trial court adopts verbatim one party's Findings of Fact and Conclusions of Law. The appeals court reviews *de novo* whether the factual findings support the district court's legal conclusions. The Court of Appeals applied *Phillips. v. Blowers* and *Slindee v. Fritch Investments, LLC* to uphold the

trial court's finding that there was no express agreement between the parties to adjust the line by practical location.
>*Cortese v. Hedin*, unpublished, A17-1201 (Minn. App. 2018)

2020 update:
Agreement to agree does not suffice for Practical Location.
>*Towley v. Wick*, unpublished, A19-0661 (Minn. App. 2019)

Disputed tree lines not sufficient to establish practical location. Other evidence not sufficient to support adverse possession of all the disputed land. Remanded for a survey and legal description of the lands adversely possessed.
>*Batton v. Hawk*, unpublished, A19-0289 (Minn. App. 2019)

Priority – Recording Act

Summary	In a dispute over who has superior rights to land, priority goes to the person who records first and without notice of a prior unrecorded claim. The Minnesota rule is often stated as "race-notice" but more correctly should be "race-without-notice."
Statute	Minn. Stat. 507.34
Limitations	None
Necessary Parties	The parties holding competing claims, and all others whose rights depend on those claims (example, mortgage or lease given by a claimant)
Elements	First in time to record; without notice of prior unrecorded claim; good faith; for valuable consideration
Burden of Proof	Person seeking priority
Standard of Proof	Preponderance
Defenses	Notice
Oddities	None
Special Torrens Note	The order in which recorded instruments are shown on the Certificate of Title is prima facie evidence of priority. *Fingerhut Corporation*

v. Suburban National Bank, 460 N.W.2d 63 (Minn. App. 1990)

Citations

A purchaser "in good faith" is one who does not have actual, implied or constructive notice of inconsistent outstanding rights held by others.
Miller v. Hennen, 438 N.W.2d 366 (Minn. 1989)

A judgment against a landowner which was docketed in August had priority over a deed to the buyer which was recorded in December. The buyer took title subject to the judgment. NOTE – this case involved Abstract property where a judgment is a lien from the time of docketing, which is different from Torrens in which a judgment is a lien from the time of recording on the certificate of title.
Nussbaumer v. Fetrow, 556 N.W.2d 595 (Minn. App. 1996)

A 38-day delay in recording a mortgage was unreasonable and cost the lender the protection of the Recording Act.
Citizens State Bank v. Raven Trading Partners, Inc., 786 N.W.2d 274 (Minn. 2010).

2018 update:

Property in a Common Interest Community (townhouse or condominium) has special priority rules. The Declaration gives the owners' association the power to levy special assessments on units to pay for annual maintenance and special projects. A special assessment is a lien on the unit. The lien may be foreclosed in the manner provided in the Declaration. The priority date of the association lien is the date of recording the Declaration. The Minnesota Common Interest Ownership Act (Chapter 515 and amendments) provides the association lien has priority over later-filed encumbrances except a "first mortgage."

Real Estate Reference Guide for Judges

In the matter of the Petition of Option One Mortgage Corporation, unpublished, A06-764 (Minn. App. 2007)

Purchase Agreement – Enjoin Cancellation or Recover Earnest Money (Residential Only)

Summary	One party to a residential purchase agreement serves a statutory notice of cancellation on the other party, who then brings a civil action to enjoin ("suspend") the cancellation, i.e., to keep the purchase agreement in place. The statutory notice of cancellation is either for cancellation with right to cure (Minn. Stat. 559.217, Subd. 3) or declaratory cancellation (Minn. Stat. 559.217, Subd. 4). This action is substantially identical to an action to enjoin the cancellation of a Contract for Deed, except that while, in the case of a Contract for Deed, only the seller can serve the statutory notice and only the buyer will seek to enjoin the cancellation, with respect to residential purchase agreement, either seller or buyer can serve the statutory notice and the opposing buyer or seller will seek to enjoin the cancellation.
Statute	Minn. Stat. 559.217 (cancellation); 559.211 (enjoin cancellation)
Limitations	Restricted to one-to-four family residential properties. Since cancellation period is typically 15 days, party seeking to enjoin cancellation must make its motion prior to expiration of that 15-day period.
Necessary Parties	Buyer and Seller but the attorney authorized to serve the cancellation notice is designated as agent for party initiating a cancellation

	notice for service of process in the action to restrain cancellation. Minn. Stat. 559.217, Subd. 8.
Elements	Under the injunction statute, Buyer may rely on any matter that would constitute a defense to the cancellation. Minn. Stat. 559.211, Subd. 1. Where the initiating party has served a notice of cancellation with right to cure under Minn. Stat. 559.217, Subd. 3, the plaintiff will seek to establish that either (a) no default occurred or (b) no unfulfilled condition existed after the date specified for fulfillment which does not by its terms cancels the purchase agreement. Where the initiating party has served a notice of declaratory cancellation under Minn. Stat. 559.217, Subd. 4, the plaintiff will seek to establish that no unfulfilled condition existed after the date specified for fulfillment which by its terms cancels the purchase agreement.
Burden of Proof	Moving party
Standard of Proof	Preponderance
Defenses	Failure of party served with notice to establish elements under *Dahlberg* (see below); failure to move for injunction prior to end of 15-day notice period.
Oddities	Court can award prevailing party filing fees, attorney fees, costs of service actually expended not to exceed $3,000.
Special	

Nathan Bissonette

Torrens Note	Proceeding Subsequent is not required because an action for an injunction does not seek to alter the Certificate of Title.
	Rule 215 Minn. Gen. R. Prac. requires an order in a civil case that affects Torrens land to be approved as to form by Examiner of Titles before presentation to court.

Citations

In evaluating requests for injunctive relief, the court will consider the five factors set forth in *Dahlberg Bros., Inc. v. Ford Motor Co.*, 137 N.W.2d 314 (Minn. 1965):

    i. The nature of the relationship of the parties prior to the dispute;
    ii. The harm likely to be suffered by either party if the injunctive relief is granted or denied;
    iii. The likelihood that one party or the other will ultimately prevail at trial;
    iv. Public policy considerations, if any; and
    v. The administrative burden on the court if injunctive relief is granted.

Due to the fact that the harm from a failure to grant the injunctive relief will mean the termination of the purchase agreement and the automatic awarding of earnest money to the party initiating the cancellation notice, Minn. Stat. 559.217, Subd. 7, courts have tended to grant injunctive relief as long as the plaintiff's claim seems meritorious. Order to suspend cancellation must be obtained within the 15-day notice period of Minn. Stat. 559.217, Subd. 4(c).
    Dimke v. Farr, 802 N.W.2d 860 (Minn. App. 2011)

Court can award prevailing party filing fees, attorney fees, costs of service actually expended not to exceed $3,000. Minn. Stat. 559.217, Subd. 6

If the notice served was declaratory cancellation, there is no right to satisfy the unfulfilled condition during the 15-day cancellation period.
>*Kalenburg v. Klein*, 847 N.W.2d 34 (Minn. App. 2014)

An unfulfilled condition is a threshold requirement under declaratory cancellation and, absent an unfulfilled condition of the purchase agreement, a declaratory cancellation is ineffective.
>*Dimke v. Farr,* 802 N.W.2d.860 (Minn. App. 2011)

If, instead of commencing an action to suspend the cancellation, the served party serves a statutory notice of counter-cancellation within the 15-day period, this has the effect of terminating the purchase agreement, but requires one of the parties to commence a civil action against the other to recover the earnest money. Despite the fact that the purchase agreement is cancelled, the court is expressly given the authority to determine which party is entitled to earnest money (regardless of who served the initial notice). Minn. Stat. 559.217, Subd. 2.

Parties generally owe duty of good faith in attempting to satisfy conditions in purchase agreement.
>*Plaisted v. Fuhr*, 367 N.W.2d 541 (Minn. App. 1985)

2018 update:
If Buyer cancels the purchase agreement and allows Seller to retain the earnest money, that payment may be an "accord and satisfaction" which bars Seller from seeking other damages from Buyer, or an "election of remedies" because Seller chose not to litigate the cancellation.
>*Lawhead v. Nixa*, unpublished, A12-0879 and A12-1547 (Minn. App. 2013).

Purchase Agreement - Specific Performance to Compel Closing

Summary	Action brought by Buyer to compel Seller to complete the sale (or, far less often, by Seller to compel Buyer to complete the sale)
Statute	None. Case can be pled as Breach of Contract seeking order to deliver the deed or as Action to Determine Adverse Claims under Chapter 559 seeking declaration that Buyer is the owner despite Seller's failure to deliver the deed
Limitations	Minn. Stat. 541.05, six years on contract claim. However, a party's right to enforce a purchase agreement may be lost if the other party can prove (by clear and convincing evidence) that the plaintiff has abandoned the purchase agreement. *Loppe v. Steiner*, 699 N.W.2d 342 (Minn. App. 2005)
Necessary Parties	Buyer and Seller
Elements	Buyer seeking to compel Seller to complete purchase must prove the terms of the contract, not be in default, and have clean hands. Seller seeking to compel Buyer to complete purchase must prove the terms of the contract, not be in default, and have clean hands

Real Estate Reference Guide for Judges

Burden of Proof	Plaintiff
Standard of Proof	Preponderance
Defenses	Contract defenses (no meeting of mind, usury, Statute of Frauds).
	Equitable defenses (laches, negligence, unclean hands, etc.). Awarding equitable relief is within the discretion of the court.
Oddities	Due to the uniqueness of real estate, generally a buyer is entitled to seek specific performance of a purchase agreement. *Schumacher v. Ihrke*, 469 N.W.2d 329 (Minn. App. 1991). The court may order the seller to issue a deed upon payment of the purchase price. In that situation, the order also should provide that if the seller fails to do so, recording a certified copy of the court's order will have the effect of a conveyance to the buyer under Rule 70 Minn. R. Civ. Pro., divesting title from Seller and vesting it in Buyer.
Special Torrens Note	If the relief sought is by the buyer to alter ownership shown on a Certificate of Title, the case must be brought as a Proceeding Subsequent.

Rule 215 Minn. Gen. R. Prac. requires an order in a civil case that affects Torrens land to be approved as to form by Examiner of Titles before presentation to court.

Citations

A seller may maintain an action against a buyer for specific performance (even if the buyer has assigned the purchase agreement).
Thompson v. Kromhout, 413 N.W.2d 884 (Minn. App. 1987)

Sellers rarely utilize the remedy of specific performance because its practical applicability is limited to a breach by a solvent purchaser of depreciating property.
Fabian v. Sather, 316 N.W.2d 10 (Minn. 1982)

2018 update:

The Supreme Court decided the second appeal following two jury trials involving an oral contract for sale of land. It doesn't matter that only money damages were sought instead of title to the land; the standard of evidence is Clear and Convincing.
Christie v. Estate of Christie, 911 N.W.2d 833 (Minn. 2018)

2022 update:

An agreement to agree is not a purchase agreement. The purported purchase agreement lacked particulars, but the correspondence indicated a willingness to make a formal agreement in the future.
Russell v. Axelson, unpublished, A21-0551 (Minn. App. 2021)

Quiet Title (Action to Determine Adverse Claims)

Summary	This is the catch-all action to determine rights in abstract land. It may be brought by a person in possession of land or by a person claiming an interest in vacant land. The action may be brought to determine rights held by a Joint Tenant or Tenant in Common.
Statute	Minn. Stat. 559.01 et. seq.
Limitations	None
Necessary Parties	All persons whose interest Plaintiff wants to divest
Elements	The elements vary depending on what specific injury is alleged
Burden of Proof	Plaintiff
Standard of Proof	Varies by legal theory
Defenses	Varies by legal theory
Oddities	The phrase "Quiet Title" technically refers only to actions brought by the government to establish clear title to mineral rights, to lands taken through tax forfeiture, or by a cemetery association or religious corporation to clear title to cemetery lots or church land. The technical phrase for other title-clearing actions is "Action to Determine Adverse Claims" but everybody uses the phrases interchangeably and Minnesota has notice pleading so use of

the wrong phrase should be disregarded by the Court.

Special
Torrens Note   Not available against Torrens land

Citations

Limitation. There is no statute of limitations on bringing this action but various other statutes may compel a result. For example, A may bring an action to determine that B has no rights in A's land. If B's claim descends from a 40-year source of title, or if B has established ownership by adverse possession, A can bring the action but will lose on the merits.

Standard of Proof and Defenses. Varies with the legal theory asserted. For example, if A brings an action to determine that B has no rights in A's land because B's lease expired, the burden is on A to prove it by a preponderance. If B counter-claims that B has established ownership of A's land through adverse possession, the burden shifts to B to prove it by clear and convincing evidence. Defenses vary according to the underlying theory of law asserted.

A quiet title action is a proceeding in equity and as such, a plaintiff who seeks to quiet title must come to court with clean hands.
   Haubrich v. U.S. Bank Nat'l Ass'n, Civ. No. 12-565 (DSD/TNL) (D. Minn. Aug. 21, 2012), affirmed 720 F.3d 979 (8th Cir. 2013)

Burden of proof is on the Plaintiff
   In *Reff v. Bank of New York Mellon,* Civ. No. 13-3415 (JNE/JSM) (D. Minn. July 24, 2014), Plaintiff asserted that once possession was shown, burden

shifted to Defendant to justify its encumbrance, which theory was rejected by the Court.

Order should include Findings of Fact and Conclusions of Law relevant to the injury sought to be relieved. For example, a quiet title action brought seeking a declaration that a mortgage does not encumber the property would include Findings to support a Conclusion why it does or doesn't. An action brought to correct a historically faulty legal description would include Findings explaining which is the wrong legal and which the right legal, a Conclusion that no named Defendant retained any rights in the property by reason of using the wrong legal, and an Order setting forth the correct legal description.

2021 update:
A person claiming title under a 'lost deed' must prove the existence and terms of the deed by clear and convincing evidence. The doctrine of laches does not affect a joint tenant's interest – it continues until terminated or conveyed. In this case, Husband and Wife owned as joint tenants, their divorce decree did not divest Wife of her interest in the property, and the only evidence of a deed from her was an ambiguous comment. Husband's claim for full ownership based on the 'lost deed' was denied for failing to meet the clear and convincing standard.
Perbix v. Hansen, 419 N.W.2d 101 (Minn. App. 1988)

2023 update:
Developer subdivided land into Lot A (landlocked) and Lot B. Lot A should have had an easement over Lot B, but the easement was omitted from the deed to Buyer. Developer sold Lot C (also landlocked) to a third party, without an easement. Owner of Lot C asserted an access easement over Lot B because of the implied easement for Lot A but poor pleadings bogged down the court, never did reach the easement issue.
Woodke v. Bracha, unpublished, A22-0892 (Minn. App. 2022)

Real Estate Reference Guide for Judges

Redemption

Summary	There is a right to "buy the land back" by redeeming after mortgage foreclosure by action, mortgage foreclosure by advertisement, or sheriff's sale to enforce a mechanic's lien or money judgment
Statute	Not a separate cause of action. Minn. Stat. 514, 550, 580, 581 (depends on underlying action)
Limitations	Certain documents must be filed before expiration of borrower's redemption period, redemption must occur within proper time period
Necessary Parties	Foreclosing entity; redeeming entities
Elements	Varies depending on underlying action
Defenses	Varies depending on underlying action
Burden of Proof	Plaintiff
Standard of Proof	Preponderance
Oddities	Owner may *reinstate* mortgage any time prior to sale by curing default. If Owner does not reinstate before sale, Owner has right to *redeem* from the sale by paying the amount bid at the sale plus fees and costs. If properly redeemed, the legal effect is as if the sale never occurred. Junior liens remain on the title. The landowner's time to redeem varies with the case: 12 months, 6 months, 2 months or 5 weeks.

Version 7.1 July 1, 2023

If the landowner fails to redeem, each junior lien holder has the right to redeem in order of priority – first lien filed gets the first week after the expiration of the land owner's redemption period; the second lien filed gets the second week; and so on. A junior lien holder who wishes to redeem must file a Notice of Intention to Redeem with the Sheriff and with the Recorder or Registrar no less than one week before the end of the landowner's redemption period and must tender the amount required to redeem to the Sheriff or to the foreclosing entity during the redeemer's assigned week (see Minn. Stat. 580.24-26). Junior lien holders who fail to redeem lose their lien – it is extinguished by the foreclosure and no longer enforceable against the land (the debt remains but the collateral is gone – it's an unsecured debt).

Redemption cases often arise from distressed property investors hoping they can acquire the property cheaply by redeeming a junior lien, and from junior creditors who claim a purported redeemer failed to follow the correct procedures; failed to tender the correct amount; or attempted to redeem during the wrong week. The cases are fact-specific. See Chapter 325N – equity stripping restrictions.

Special Torrens Note	Rule 215 Minn. Gen. R. Prac. requires order in a civil case that affects Torrens land to be approved as to form by Examiner of Titles before presentation to court.

Real Estate Reference Guide for Judges

Citations

No matter how we got to the Sheriff's Sale (mortgage foreclosure, Writ of Execution, Mechanic's Lien, etc.), all redemptions proceed under Minn. Stat. 580.23 - 27.

The Owner doesn't have to file anything before exercising redemption rights.
>Minn. Stat. 580.23

Junior Creditors must complete all of the following steps no less than one week prior to the expiration of the Owner's redemption period:
> (1) record with each County Recorder (if the land is abstract) and Registrar of Titles (if the land is Torrens) in the county where the foreclosed land is located, a notice of the creditor's intention to redeem; (2) record with each County Recorder and Registrar of Titles where the notice of the creditor's intention to redeem is recorded, all documents necessary to create the lien on the foreclosed lands and to evidence the creditor's ownership of the lien, including a copy of any money judgment necessary to create the lien; and
>
> (3) after complying with clauses (1) and (2), deliver to the Sheriff who conducted the foreclosure sale a copy of each of the documents required to be recorded under clauses (1) and (2), with the office, date and time of filing for record stated on the first page of each document.
>>Minn. Stat. 580.24

A person redeems by tendering the payment required by law (set by Minn. Stat. 582.03) and copies of the above items to the person receiving redemption (generally the Sheriff).
>Minn. Stat. 580.25

The issue is likely to come before the Court on a dispute over who is entitled to redeem, for what amount, and in what order and, perhaps, for damages.

A junior creditor redeemed property from a senior creditor in a foreclosure proceeding and later claimed that the senior creditor's mortgage was fraudulent.
    Parker v. St. Martin, 55 N.W. 113 (1893)

Redemption requires substantial compliance with the statute, not strict compliance.
    Sieve v. Rosar, 613 N.W.2d 789 (Minn. App. 2000)

A District Court Judgment is a lien on abstract property from the time of docketing the judgment under Minn. Stat. 548.09; but for redemption purposes, a Transcript of Judgment must be recorded and delivered to the Sheriff.
    Northern Realty Ventures, LLC, v. Minnesota Housing Finance Agency, 748 N.W.2d 296 (Minn. App. 2008)

Order should include Findings of Fact as to identity of everyone holding an interest, their respective priorities, and the dates of important acts such as filing, delivering and tendering, and Conclusions of Law should address who was entitled to redeem, who timely redeemed from whom, and who is entitled to own the property.

Real Estate Reference Guide for Judges

Late Filers – We're Aware of the Issue, But Nobody Knows the Answer

The one-week-prior-to-redemption requirement was added in 2008 specifically to give enough time for the Sheriff and junior creditors to know who had the right to redeem, and in what order. Two troubling situations frequently arise but the law is unsettled.

First, a party may assign its rights in the property (a lien, for example) and also may attempt to assign its Notice of Intent to Redeem on that lien. The assignment may occur less than one-week-prior, so the Assignee cannot timely record its own Notice of Intent to Redeem.

Second, a party may claim a new interest in the property that arose less than one-week-prior, such as a Mechanic's Lien for work recently done or a mortgage recently given, for which the claimant cannot timely record its Notice of Intent to Redeem.

Initially, there is the matter of standing to object. In *Real Estate Equity Strategies, LLC, v. I.R.S.,* 540 F.3d 860 (8th Cir., 2008), the Court held that the only person who may attack a redemption that is fair on the face of the record, but wrongful in fact, is the purchaser at the Sheriff' Sale or a junior creditor who attempted to redeem in accordance with the statutes. In the absence of such objection, the Court could overlook the defects in the redemption.

Secondarily, if objection to redemption is raised, there are two lines of cases addressing defective redemptions: the "strict compliance" line and the "substantial compliance" line.

The "strict compliance" line of cases includes *Petition of Brainerd National Bank,* 383 N.W.2d 284 (Minn. 1986); *Greybow-Daniels Co. v. Pinotti,* 255 N.W.2d 405 (Minn. 1997); *Northern Realty Ventures v. Minnesota Housing Finance Agency,* 748 N.W.2d 296

(Minn. App. 2008); see also *Real Estate Equity Strategies, LLC, v. I.R.S.,* 540 F.3d 860 (8th Cir., 2008).

The "substantial compliance" line of cases includes *Tinkcom v. Lewis,* 21 Minn. 132 (Minn. 1874), *Sieve v. Rosar,* 613 N.W.2d 789 (Minn. App. 2000) and *Timeline, LLC v. Williams Holdings #3, LLC,* 698 N.W.2d 181 (Minn. App. 2005).

The decision as to which line of cases controls appears to turn on these factors:

> All redeeming creditors must strictly comply with the statutory requirements to document the existence of their right to redeem, such as recording evidence of lien.
>
> Redeeming creditors must strictly comply with timing, tender, payment and post-redemption recording requirements when failure to do so prejudices junior creditors.
>
> Redeeming creditors may substantially comply with tender, payment and post-redemption recording requirements when failure to do so does not prejudice junior creditors.

There are no cases in either the "strict compliance" or the "substantial compliance" line of cases that addresses failure to record one-week-prior and, thus, there are no cases addressing the likely defenses to failure to comply with the statute: impossibility and public purpose.

Your Examiner is aware of one Hennepin County District Court case, *Mortgage Electronic Registration Systems, Inc., v. NJD Properties, LLC, et. al,* 27-CV-10-27935, in which Hon. Margaret Daly granted summary judgment upholding the senior redeeming creditor's redemption despite its having failed to meet the one-week-prior deadline to file the Notice of Intent to Redeem. The Court found the defects in the senior redeeming creditor's redemption did

Real Estate Reference Guide for Judges

not prejudice the junior redeeming creditor who had, itself, failed to strictly comply.

Un-adjudicated heirs – We're Aware of the Issue, But Nobody Knows the Answer

The holdings in *Laymon v. Minnesota Premier Properties, LLC*, 913 N.W.2d 449 (Minn. 2018) and *In the Matter of the Petition of Beachside I Homeowners Ass'n,* 802 N.W.2d 771 (Minn. App. 2011) confirmed the common law rule that real estate is never unowned; instead, title passes at the moment of death, subject to administration by the probate court. *Laymon* specifically says the heir or devisee has sufficient title to redeem from foreclosure.

The question is what the heir or devisee must do to establish that right. Can an un-adjudicated heir redeem as "owner," or must she first obtain an order from the probate court adjudicating her (and perhaps others) as a legitimate heir/devisee? If an unadjudicated heir/devisee conveys her interest to a property flipper, can he redeem as "owner" even though there may be other heirs/devisees who did not convey? Does he redeem only her interest or all their interests? Does he solely own fee title, or does he take title in trust for the others?

Suppose title is held by A, a single woman. She dies, her estate is not probated. B, claiming to be the heir of A, gives a deed to C, a distressed property investor. Later C, claiming to be the owner on the strength of the deed from B, tenders money to the Sheriff to redeem from the foreclosure.

But what if A had a Will specifically excluding worthless son B and specifically leaving her real estate to Ducks Unlimited? Did the deed from disinherited worthless son B to Flipper C convey anything? Is the redemption valid? Can Ducks Unlimited attempt to redeem, claiming to be the un-adjudicated devisee?

2018 update:

>Title to land passes to the heirs/devisees at the moment of death, subject to administration of the estate by the Personal Representative. An heir or devisee has an interest sufficient to redeem from foreclosure.

Laymon v. Minnesota Premier Properties, LLC, 913 N.W.2d 449 (Minn. 2018)

2020 update:
An owner can assign mortgage foreclosure redemption rights separate from fee ownership. Redemption by the assignee is effective and upon redemption, fee title belongs to the redeemer, not the former owner who reserved fee title from the assignment.
Schumacher v. KMLE, Inc., unpublished, A19-0972 (Minn. App. 2020)

The holder of a sheriff's certificate has no standing to object to redemption by assignee of the mortgagor.
Plaza Holdings, LLC v. Jeffrey Wirth, unpublished, A17-1533 (Minn. App. 2018).

2021 update:
Minn. Stat. 582.032 provides that the court may reduce the owner's redemption period to five weeks on an expedited basis, for certain abandoned properties. The statute requires the complaint to name one of "the mortgagor, or the mortgagor's personal representatives or assigns of record, as defendant." Most Examiners of Title opine this provision precludes reduction of the redemption period in an 'unknown heirs' case because there is nobody to name as defendant and insufficient time to publish the Summons to obtain personal jurisdiction. One court allowed the case to proceed where the lender served all the decedent's children who were named in the obituary and none of them appeared in opposition. This holding is not precedential, and the authors do not recommend it.
Paramount Investment Group, LLC v. the unknown heirs of Kenneth C. Wieden, et. al., Court File 62-CV-21-885 (Minnesota Second Judicial District, 2021)

Real Estate Reference Guide for Judges

2023 update:

District court dispute between two distressed property investors – Resolution and Equihance - which both wanted to redeem from foreclosure as junior creditors following expiration of record owner's redemption period. A money judgment against the record owner was entered and assigned to Resolution. A second judgment against the record owner was entered and judgment creditor gave an Assignment to Equihance, but the Assignment was not docketed in district court until after the statutory deadline prescribed in Minn. Stat. 580.24. Held: Equihance failed to strictly comply with the requirements to establish its right to redeem.

Resolution Home Buyers LLC v. Equihance Partners, LLC, District Court File 62-CV-22-557 (2022)

Homeowner was foreclosed, failed to redeem from foreclosure. Junior Creditor redeemed using a judgment, then conveyed to new owner. Homeowner challenged foreclosure and lost, then challenged redemption in a separate proceeding on grounds the judgment was not against her but against a person with a similar name, and the redeeming judgment creditor had not been made a party to the case. Held: The judgment creditor was not a necessary party because it no longer had an interest in the lands and homeowner lacked standing to challenge the redemption.

In re Rossman, unpublished, A22-0141 (Minn. App. 2022)

Parents deeded the family farm to one child subject to liens in favor of siblings. In dispute over the effective date of the liens, court found the deed ambiguous and reformed it. Good discussion of the requirements for reformation.

Stueckrath v. Stueckrath, unpublished, A22-1188 (Minn. App. 2023)

This 2016 case was found while researching another matter. It is included because it contains a helpful explanation of the

court's reasoning. Held: A party cannot waive its statutory right to redemption.
> *U.S. Bank National Association, as Trustee, v. RBP Realty, LLC*, 888 N.W.2d 699 (Minn. App. 2016)

The Sheriff's Certificate was prepared on a typewriter. The sale amount was unclear. Owner conveyed to Investor who attempted to redeem by tendering $4,600 to the Sheriff rather than $44,600 which was the correct sale price, and upon rejection by the Sheriff, failed to tender the full amount before the expiration of the redemption period. Held: the amount required to redeem is the amount for which the property was sold at the foreclosure sale, not the amount shown on the Sheriff's Certificate of Sale. Investor should have tendered the full amount then litigated the amount due.
> *Platinum Edge Properties, LLC v. Federal National Mortgage Association*, unpublished, A22-1576 (Minn. App. 2023)

Reformation of a Document

Summary	The doctrine of reformation allows a district court to alter or amend a written agreement to reflect the parties' true intentions at the time they entered into the agreement.
Statute	None, usually pled as Declaratory Judgment under Chapter 555
Limitations	None
Necessary Parties	Parties to the instrument being reformed, landowner of record, lien holders, occupants and other persons affected by changing the instrument (example, if Tenants-in-Common deed is reformed to Joint Tenants, then the heirs-at-law of each tenant will be 'disinherited' so they must be made parties).
Elements	There was a valid agreement between the parties expressing their real intentions;
	The written instrument failed to express the real intentions of the parties; and,
	This failure was due to a mutual mistake of the parties, or a unilateral mistake accompanied by fraud or inequitable conduct by the other party.

Nathan Bissonette

Burden of Proof	Plaintiff to prove each element of a reformation claim
Standard of Proof	"Clear and consistent, unequivocal and convincing"
Defenses	Document does reflect the parties' true intent, should not be reformed, or equitable defenses (laches, negligence, unclean hands, etc.)
Oddities	If reformation is granted, the document is retroactively reformed, as if it had always been that way: reformation is *nunc pro tunc*.
	Often pled as part of a Foreclosure by Action (to retroactively cure a defect in a mortgage) or for Specific Performance (to clarify terms of agreement).
Special Torrens Note	If the relief sought is to alter a document shown on a Certificate of Title, the case must be brought as a Proceeding Subsequent.
	Rule 215 Minn. Gen. R. Prac. requires an order in a civil case that affects Torrens land to be approved as to form by Examiner of Titles before presentation to court.

Citations

   The doctrine of reformation allows a district court to alter or amend a written agreement to reflect the parties' true intentions at the time they entered into the agreement.

Real Estate Reference Guide for Judges

Jablonski v. Mutual Serv. Cas. Ins. Co., 408 N.W.2d 854 (Minn. 1987)

"Reformation of a written agreement is available when parties reached an agreement, attempted to reduce it to writing, but failed to express [the agreement] correctly in the writing."
> *SCI Minn. Funeral Services., Inc. v. Washburn-McReavy Funeral Corp.*, 779 N.W.2d 865 (Minn. App. 2010), *affirmed,* 795 N.W.2d 855 (Minn. 2011)

To prevail, a plaintiff seeking reformation must prove the following elements of the claim:
> there was a valid agreement between the parties expressing their real intentions;
> the written instrument failed to express the real intentions of the parties; and
> this failure was due to a mutual mistake of the parties, or a unilateral mistake accompanied by fraud or inequitable conduct by the other party.
>> *Nichols v. Shelard Nat'l Bank,* 294 N.W.2d 730 (Minn. 1980)

The burden of proof is on the plaintiff to prove each element of a reformation claim. The standard of proof is "by evidence which is clear and consistent, unequivocal and convincing."
> *Nichols v. Shelard Nat'l Bank,* 294 N.W.2d 730 (Minn. 1980)

2019 update:
> A deed is effective upon delivery. Buyer must be alive to take delivery. A deed signed by Seller after death of Buyer does not transfer title to Buyer, nor to his estate. Deed may be reformed, or constructive trust imposed.
>> *In re Estate of Savich,* 671 N.W. 2d 746 (Minn. App. 2003)

Version 7.1   July 1, 2023

But a deed given to the PR of an estate to correct defects in the chain of title is okay.
> *In re Estate of Harold E. Farnes,* A18-0036, unpublished, (Minn. App. 2019)

2020 update:
Deed reformed to include an omitted easement.
> *Isanti Pines Tree Farm LLC v. Swanson,* unpublished, A19-0749, A19-1585 (Minn. App. 2020).

2021 update:
Two mortgages given, one for each parcel, but legal descriptions were reversed, and then one mortgage was satisfied. Mortgages were reformed to correct the legal descriptions and reinstate the wrongly satisfied mortgage as a lien on the land.
> *Ameriquest Mortgage Company v. Hanson,* unpublished, A08-0282 (Minn. App. 2009)

Restrictive Covenants (30-year law)

Summary	Private (non-government) restrictive covenants shouldn't burden land forever. By statute, some restrictions become unenforceable after a time.
Statute	Minn. Stat. 500.20 ("Defeasible Estates," horrible name, who'd ever look there?)
Limitation	30 years has passed since last recorded renewal. No removal limitation thereafter but six-year limit on breach of conditions subsequent.
Necessary Parties	Land owner, holder of encumbrance to be removed, persons affected by the removal
Elements 500.20	Vary by encumbrance – see Minn. Stat.
Burden of Proof	Plaintiff
Standard of Proof	Preponderance
Defenses	Does not fall under statute; time has not elapsed
Oddities	Cannot use to cut off rights of re-entry, condominium or co-op documents, party wall agreements, government restrictions – see Minn. Stat. 500.20
Special Torrens Note	If the relief sought primarily involves an alteration to a Certificate of Title (example, omitting the memorial of Restrictive

Covenants), the action must be brought as a Proceeding Subsequent under Minn. Stat. 508.71, Subd. 2. Rule 215 Minn. Gen. R. Prac. requires an order in a civil case that affects Torrens land to be approved as to form by Examiner of Titles before presentation to court.

Citations

"Ancient records shall not fetter the marketability of real estate."
> *Wichelman v. Messner*, 83 N.W.2d 800 (Minn. 1957). Interplay between 40-year law and 30-year law explained.

Restrictive covenant unenforceable after 30 years and no renewal filed.
> *Matter of Turners Crossroad Development Co.*, 277 N.W.2d 364 (Minn. 1979)

Restrictive covenants are contracts, reviewed *de novo* to give effect to the parties' intent.
> *Morgan Square, LLC v. Lakeville Land, Ltd.*, A12-2271 unpublished, (Minn. App. 2013)

2020 update:

Duluth Automobile Club obtained a golf course, merged into Minnesota State Auto Association, and then filed restrictive covenants on the title to the land requiring it to be used as a golf course. New owner sought to remove the restrictive covenants as expired under the 30-year law (Minn. Stat. 500.20, Subd 2(a). Held: the restrictions have expired. The 30-year law is retroactive to cover agreements recorded at any time in the past (with certain exceptions in the statute).
> *In re The Auto Club Group v. Anderson,* unpublished, A19-0327, (Minn. App.2019)

Real Estate Reference Guide for Judges

Restrictive covenants can be enforced by temporary injunction.
Kossick v. DiamondRock Development, LLC, unpublished, A19-2043, (Minn. App. 2020)

Nathan Bissonette

Riparian Rights

Summary	The owner of land adjoining water has the right to use the water, called "riparian rights." Cases arise from interference with riparian rights.
Statute	None
Limitations	None
Necessary Parties	Riparian owner, interfering party, State of Minnesota
Elements	Varies with legal theory
Burden of Proof	Plaintiff
Standard of Proof	Preponderance
Defenses	Varies with legal theory
Oddities	The State of Minnesota has regulatory authority over public waters. The interplay between the State's authority and landowner's rights is complex. The State should be named as Defendant in every riparian rights case.
Special	

Real Estate Reference Guide for Judges

Torrens Note   If the relief sought is to alter a document shown on a Certificate of Title, the case must be brought as a Proceeding Subsequent.

Rule 215 Minn. Gen. R. Prac. requires an order in a civil case that affects Torrens land to be approved as to form by Examiner of Titles before presentation to court.

Citations

A riparian owner "has a right to make such use of the lake over its entire surface, in common with all other abutting owners, provided such use is reasonable and does not unduly interfere with the exercise of similar rights on the part of other abutting owners."
     Johnson v. Seifert, 100 N.W.2d 689 (Minn. 1960)

The owner of riparian land enjoys the right of exclusive access to water that is directly in front of his or her waterfront property, and "title extends to the low-water mark."
     State, by Head v. Slotness, 185 N.W. 2d 530 (Minn. 1971)

Interference with riparian rights is an appropriate subject for injunctive relief.
     Petraborg v. Zontelli, 15 N.W.2d 174 (Minn. 1944)

When there is continuing and repeated interference with real property rights, the law presumes irreparable damage and inadequate legal remedies.
     Whittaker v. Stangvick, 111 N.W. 295 (Minn. 1907)

Dock regulations cannot completely deny riparian rights.
     Lake Minnetonka Conservation District v. Canning, A05-1811, unpublished (Minn. App. 2006)

"Who owns the land where the water used to be?" is a frequently litigated question, as lakes recede and streams change course. The answer is not straightforward.

Navigable versus Non-Navigable

At the time of Minnesota's admission to the Union on May 11, 1858, the beds of all navigable waters within its boundaries came under ownership of the state, while non-navigable waters remained under ownership of the federal government.
State v. Adams, 89 N.W.2d 661 (Minn. 1957)

Streams and lakes are considered navigable waters when "they are used, or are susceptible of use, in their ordinary and natural condition, as highways for commerce, whether by steamboats, sailing vessels, or flatboats, and even though occasional difficulties are encountered in connection therewith."
State v. Longyear Holding Co., 29 N.W.2d 657 (Minn. 1947)

Navigability for this purpose is determined by federal law. *U.S. v. Holt State Bank,* 270 U.S. 49 (1926). The controlling factors and cases are:

(1) That the capability of use rather than the extent or manner thereof by the public for transportation and commerce affords the true criteria of navigability of waters, *U. S. v. Holt State Bank*, supra;
(2) that a watercourse may be navigable notwithstanding serious obstructions occasioned by natural barriers such as rapids and sand bars, *The Montello*, 87 U.S. 430 (1874);
(3) that the true test of navigability of waters does not depend upon the mode in which the commerce thereon is conducted or the difficulties attending it, *U. S. v. State of Utah*, 283 U.S. 64 (1931);

(4) that the uses and purposes to which waters may be put to meet the test of navigability vary from the carrying of ocean liners to the floating out of logs, *U. S. v. Appalachian Elec. Power Co.*, 311 U.S. 377 (1940)
(5) that the density of traffic on waters may vary widely, but the tests must take these variations into account, *U. S. v. Appalachian Elec. Power Co.*, supra;
(6) that a waterway otherwise suitable for navigation is not barred from that classification merely because artificial aids are required before commercial navigation may be undertaken, *U. S. v. Appalachian Elec. Power Co.* supra,
(7) that, once a waterway is determined to be navigable, it remains so, *U. S. v. Appalachian Elec. Power Co.* supra; E*conomy Light & Power Co. v. U. S.*, 256 U.S. 113 (1921)
(8) that temporary abandonment or disuse of a waterway as a highway of commerce does not terminate its navigable status, since subsequent improvements may restore its usefulness, *Economy Light & Power Co. v. U. S.*, supra; and
(9) that artificial obstructions such as lumber and dams which may be abated by exercise of public authority do not prevent a stream from being navigable in law. *Economy Light & Power Co. v. U. S.*, supra.

NOTE: Under federal law, the lake bed of a non-navigable lake remained the property of the United States and was not conveyed to the State of Minnesota upon admission to the Union. But the State has statutory regulatory authority over ALL waters and therefore ***should be named as defendant*** to confirm the State of Minnesota's interest.

Meandered versus Non-Meandered

When the land surveyors doing the Original Government Survey in the 1800's reached a small body of water, they surveyed across it. That lake is non-meandered. When they reached the edge of a larger body of water, they walked around it. That lake is meandered.

Non-meandered lakes lie on someone's land. The owner owns the land under the water, same as a puddle in a low spot in your backyard. Lands adjacent to meandered waters carry title to the water's edge but not to the land under the water. *Patton and Palomar on Titles*, Section 117.

The general concept of riparian ownership of lands adjacent to meandered non-navigable water is that the landowner's rights extend to the water's edge. In a sense, the boundary "chases the water" moving back and forth as the water level rises and falls.

"A meander line is not a line of boundary, but one designed to point out the sinuosity of the bank or shore, and a means of ascertaining the quantity of land in the fraction which is to be paid for by the purchaser." *Whitaker v. Bride,* 197 U. S. 510 at 512 (1905)

A plat to the meander line is, by operation of law, a plat to the water's edge, unless the platter manifested a contrary intent. *Sherwin v. Bitzer,* 106 N.W. 1046 (Minn. 1906). The case law deals with plats, not registered land surveys, likely because registered land surveys are a recent creature of the Torrens system of land registration and less common than plats. There are no cases treating subdivision by registered land survey differently from subdivision by plat.

Drawing riparian lines

Early case-law provided that riparian owners' lot lines were extended to the geographical center of the lake regardless of deep spots. *Scheifert v. Briegel,* 96 N.W. 44 (Minn. 1903). When the extended lot lines didn't point at the geographical center, the extended lines bent toward the geographical center. The bend point was the meander line. *State v. Adams*, 89 N. W. 2d 661 (Minn. 1957), footnote 18. At the time of those early cases, it was public policy in Minnesota to drain swamps and divert waters to increase tillable lands and to reduce mosquito habitat. The result was dried-up lakes that were never coming back. In those cases, there was no water's edge to chase and never would be. Dividing up the dry lakebed on a simple geographical basis made sense.

Long, narrow lakes may not have an easily determined geographical center, or using it may create unusable burdensome tracts. In those cases, the bend point for extended lot lines still was the meander line but the Court extended those lines perpendicular to the thread of the lake, similar to a stream. *Rooney v. County of Stearns*, 153 N.W. 858 (Minn. 1915)

In 1940, a University of Minnesota law review article argued that the geographical center rule was inconsistent with the general principle of "chasing the water" when applied to lakes that had not completely dried up. The author argued for a fair and equitable division that preserved riparian owners' rights on a case-by-case basis. *Title, Points and Lines in Lakes and Streams*, Edward S. Bade, 24 Minn. L. Rev. 305, 1939-1940. This analysis was found persuasive by the Court of Appeals, which held that:

> "In order to determine the extent of riparian rights, riparian boundaries must be ascertained. Minnesota case law does not endorse a specific method for drawing riparian boundaries, although a method is described in Edward S. Bade, *Title, Points & Lines in Lakes & Streams*, 24 Minn. L. Rev. 305, 306-07 (1940). Bade rejects a "rule of straight projection" to arrive at riparian rights and suggests a more proportionate method based on the shape of the lake. *Id.* at 341.

> While no single method applies in every case, what remains important is that the boundaries are drawn in a fair and equitable manner. *See, e.g., Rooney v. County of Stearns*, 153 N.W. 858 (Minn. 1915); *Scheifert v. Briegel*, 96 N.W. 44 (Minn. 1903)."
>
> *Lake Minnetonka Conservation District v. Miles B. Canning*, No. A05-1811, unpublished, (Minn. App. 2006)

2019 update:

Riparian rights extend to the water. If the water recedes, Riparian Owner may cross intervening dry land to reach the water, without committing trespass.

Xu v. Sterling, A18-1741, unpublished (Minn. App. 2019)

2021 update:

The owner of land across a platted street from the lake has riparian rights. [Note: this holding is fact-specific. An 'edge street' in a subdivision which is platted to the water's edge runs all the way to the water. Since the City only has an easement in the street, the adjacent landowner owns the land under the street all the way to the water. In that situation, there is no owner on the lake side of the street to claim competing riparian rights. In contrast, an 'edge street' which is platted to the meander line or some other line short of the water's edge may leave a strip of land between the street and the water. In that case, the off-shore owner would not have riparian rights because the lakeside owner has them.]

Carlson v. Township of Livonia, unpublished, A20-0993 (Minn. App. 2021)

Real Estate Reference Guide for Judges

The plat dedicated a 'fire lane' to the city. The dedication gave the city an easement over the fire lane, with fee title owned by the adjacent landowners. The fire lane ends at the water's edge. The city's easement entitles it to riparian rights in the lake. But the city's riparian rights flowing from its easement do not supersede the adjacent landowners' riparian rights. The exercise of riparian rights must be reasonable and must not unduly interfere with the exercise of similar rights on the part of other owners.

Schussler v. City of the Village of Minnetonka Beach, unpublished, A20-0919 (Minn. App. 2021)

2023 update:

Second appeal on the Carlson case, above, affirms the main points. Carlsons own a platted lot. Their lot abuts an edge street. Across the street is Lake Freemont. Title to the lands under the street belong to the owners of the platted lot (Carlson) which entitled them to riparian rights in the lake including the right to place a dock. The fact the street is unimproved and designated minimum maintenance does not make it private property which they can block and does not entitle them to exclusive riparian rights as to that bit of lakeshore. Riparian rights are shared with all other riparian owners on the lake.

Carlson v. Township of Livonia, unpublished, A22-0020 (Minn. App. 2022)

Slander of Title

Summary	A false statement about land that causes the landowner loss (example: mortgage recorded on the wrong parcel)
Statute	None, usually pled as declaratory judgment, Chapter 555 or Action to Determine Adverse Claims under Chapter 559
Limitations	Two years, Minn. Stat. 541.07 (1)
Necessary Parties	The persons who caused the false statement to be published. Query whether it might include re-publication (example, newspaper that published Notice of Foreclosure of falsely recorded mortgage)
Elements	A false statement concerning the real property owned by the plaintiff; the false statement was published to others; the false statement was published maliciously; and the publication of the false statement concerning title to the property caused the plaintiff pecuniary loss in the form of special damages.
Burden of Proof	Plaintiff
Standard of Proof	Preponderance
Defenses	Truth; statement did not concern the real estate; was not published to others; not published maliciously.

Real Estate Reference Guide for Judges

Plaintiffs must establish that the alleged false statement was relied upon to cause Plaintiff's loss. *Welk v. GMAC Mortgage, LLC*, 850 F.Supp.2d 976 (D. Minn. 2102)

Oddities

"Special Damages" can include attorney's fees in bringing the action to remove the slander. *Paidar v. Hughes*, 615 N.W.2d 276 (Minn. 2000)

Special Torrens Note

If the relief sought is to alter a document shown on a Certificate of Title, the case must be brought as a Proceeding Subsequent.

Rule 215 Minn. Gen. R. Prac. requires an order in a civil case that affects Torrens land to be approved as to form by Examiner of Titles before presentation to court.

Citations

The elements are:
(1) there was a false statement concerning the real property owned by the plaintiff;
(2) the false statement was published to others;
(3) the false statement was published maliciously; and
(4) the publication of the false statement concerning title to the property caused the plaintiff pecuniary loss in the form of special damages.
Paidar v. Hughes, 615 N.W.2d 276 (Minn. 2000)

The filing of an instrument known to be inoperative is a false statement that, if done maliciously, constitutes slander of title.
Kelly v. First State Bank of Rothsay, 177 N.W. 347 (Minn. 1920)

"Maliciously" requires reckless disregard for the truth or falsity of the matter, despite a high degree of awareness of probable falsity.
Brickner v. One Land Dev. Co., 742 N.W.2d 706 (Minn. App. 2007)

"Special Damages" can include attorney's fees in bringing the action to remove the slander.
Paidar v. Hughes, 615 N.W.2d 276 (Minn. 2000)

Additionally, plaintiffs claiming damages because of a false statement in a recorded document must establish that they actually relied on the false statement in that document when incurring damages. Without reliance or damages, a slander of title claim must fail.
Welk v. GMAC Mortgage, LLC, 850 F.Supp.2d 976 (D. Minn. 2102)

The Order should include findings on each element and specific findings of evidence showing Malice and amount of Special Damages.

2019 update:
Elements explained, good faith filing of Notice of Lis Pendens does not slander title.
Drydahl v. McDowell, A18-1301, unpublished (Minn. App. 2018)

2023 update:
This 2009 case was found while researching another matter. It is included because it contains a helpful explanation of the court's reasoning. Held: There was sufficient support for the district court's finding of malice with the slander of title claim citing non-lienable items included in the mechanic's lien and fraudulent billing practices.
LeMaster Construction, Inc. v. Woeste, unreported, A-08-0956 (Minn. App. 2009)

Real Estate Reference Guide for Judges

Sovereign Citizen Claims

We generally see these asserted when borrowers are defending mortgage foreclosures by asserting they are not subject to the law, or the law is unconstitutional, such as:

"Accept the Deed"
There is an on-line video entitled "No Longer Tenants – Accept the Deed" that confused many Sovereign Citizens. The author asserts that when a seller gives a buyer a deed, it conveys only "marketable" title, but if the buyer "accepts" the deed by filing a written acceptance document in the land records, then the buyer's title is converted to "Good" title and sheds all encumbrances *including the mortgage*. It's pure nonsense and has no basis in Minnesota law.

Allodial title/Patent Title Holder
Sovereign citizens argue their title is "allodial" title which, by definition, is free from all claims; therefore, the mortgage does not encumber the land and cannot be foreclosed.

Under ancient English law, all land was owned by the King, who could grant lands to favored subjects and revoke land grants at his whim. Title to lands was never secure from the King. The Founders, having only just thrown off that system, determined not to repeat it. Grants of land from the United States government cannot be revoked at whim – they are "allodial" meaning they are free from claims by the United States; BUT, those lands can be later encumbered by the owner according to the laws of the state where located. Allodial lands do not remain free of encumbrances created by the title holder. The mortgage cannot be avoided by this claim.

No Debt (gold and silver specie)
The fact that no debt is owed is a legitimate defense to mortgage foreclosure. But Sovereign Citizens argue they "owe no debt" by the following reasoning: A debt is a promise to repay 'money;' 'money' is defined in the Constitution as gold or silver coins; the lender did not give anyone gold or silver but merely created a bookkeeping

entry in its ledger and exchanged electrons with the seller's bank; the lender's failure to pay 'money' is a failure of consideration for the promise to repay 'money;' lack of consideration voids the Promissory Note; no debt means there is no basis for foreclosure. Your Examiner is not aware of any court that has accepted this reasoning.

There are endless variations, such as calling oneself by an odd name to avoid submitting to the supremacy of the federal government or insisting that a United States flag with gold fringe converts the proceeding to a court-martial. The internet is a rich source to debunk these claims.

Nonconsensual Common Law Lien
Some unhappy litigants record a "common law lien" against public officials who fail to grant the requested relief. See Minn. Stat. 514.99 for removal procedures.

2021 update:
>Plaintiff's claims to be a sovereign citizen and therefore not subject to the jurisdiction of the court nor subject to criminal laws were frivolous and utterly without merit.
>*Leon Henry Carter-Bey, III v. Lefler and Schnell,* Memorandum and Order, Civ. No. 21-1406 (PAM/ECW), United States District Court, D. Minnesota, August 10, 2021

Specific Performance to compel sale closing

Summary	Action brought to compel Seller to complete the sale
Statute	None. Case can be pled as breach of contract seeking order to deliver the deed; or as Action to Determine Adverse Claims under Chapter 559 seeking declaration that Buyer is the owner despite Seller's failure to deliver the deed
Limitations	Minn. Stat. 541.05, six years on contract claim
Necessary Parties	Buyer and Seller
Elements	Seller seeking to compel Buyer to complete purchase must prove the terms of the contract, not be in default, and have clean hands
Burden of Proof	Plaintiff
Standard of Proof	Preponderance

Defenses	Impossibility of Performance is a common Seller defense (e.g. purchase agreement calls for clean title but Seller cannot provide clean title).
	Contract defenses (no meeting of mind, usury, Statute of Frauds).
	Equitable defenses (laches, negligence, unclean hands, etc.). Awarding equitable relief is within the discretion of the court.
Oddities	Due to the uniqueness of real estate, generally a buyer is entitled to seek specific performance of a purchase agreement. *Schumacher v. Ihrke*, 469 N.W.2d 329 (Minn. App. 1991). The court may order the seller to issue a deed upon payment of the purchase price. In that situation, the order also should provide that if the seller fails to do so, recording a certified copy of the court's order will have the effect of a conveyance to the buyer under Rule 70 Minn. R. Civ. Pro., divesting title from Seller and vesting it in Buyer.
	Non-performing party may attempt statutory cancellation while case is pending. A restraining order to maintain the status quo might be wise. Minn. Stat. 559.211-217
Special Torrens Note	If the relief sought is to alter ownership shown on a Certificate of Title, the case must be brought as a Proceeding Subsequent.
	Rule 215 Minn. Gen. R. Prac. requires an order in a civil case that affects Torrens land

Real Estate Reference Guide for Judges

to be approved as to form by Examiner of Titles before presentation to court.

Citations

The value of land can change over time and that can turn a good deal into a bad one. Specific Performance is equitable relief in which the Court orders the parties to complete the deal.

A seller may demand Specific Performance when the buyer wants to back out of a purchase because the land is no longer worth what the buyer agreed to pay for it. A seller seeking Specific Performance to compel the buyer to complete the purchase must not be in default at the time performance is due.
Friede v. Pool, 14 N.W.2d 454 (Minn. 1944)

A buyer may demand Specific Performance when the seller wants to back out of a sale because the land is worth more than the seller agreed to take for it. Specific Performance is an equitable remedy available to either side, but the party requesting equitable relief must have "clean hands."

Awarding Specific Performance is within the discretion of the court.
Thompson v. Kromhout, 413 N.W.2d 884 (Minn. App. 1987)

Every parcel of land is slightly different and that makes it unique. A buyer may demand Specific Performance when a seller won't deliver title to the parcel agreed upon, but instead wishes to substitute another parcel. Seller's defense will be there's nothing special about the first parcel so other land can be substituted, perhaps with money to make up the difference. The Court must decide which is true.

Auntie Ruth's Furry Friends' Home Away From Home, Ltd., v. GCC Property Management, LLC, A10-993, unpublished (Minn. App. 2010)

2021 update:

The Buyer's abandonment of the purchase agreement is an affirmative defense the Seller must plead in her Answer to an action for Specific Performance. Abandonment must be proven by Clear and Convincing evidence.
Loppe v. Steiner, 699 N.W.2d 342 (Minn. App. 2005)

2022 update:

Not a statute of frauds case – a lack of consideration case – but one which goes to the validity of a purported conveyance. A dying woman gave a Warranty Deed to her grandson. He did not pay for the property. The Personal Representative of her estate challenged the deed. No consideration is necessary to support a Quit Claim Deed, but consideration is required for a Warranty Deed. Since none was paid, the deed was void.
TC Inv. Grp. v. King, unpublished, A21-0531 (Minn. App. 2021)

Real Estate Reference Guide for Judges

Statute of Frauds

Summary	Not a separate cause of action, but a consideration in any action involving title to real estate.
Statute	Minn. Stat. 513.04 is the Statute of Frauds (poor name: should be the Statute for Prevention of Frauds). The essence is that to prevent fraudulent claims to land, almost all conveyances must be in writing and signed by the landowner. Arises in cases involving Adverse Possession, Practical Location, Registration of Boundaries, Reformation of Documents, Initial Registration and Proceedings Subsequent.
Limitations	No specific statute, use statute of limitations for underlying cause of action
Necessary Parties	Everyone whose interests would be affected by the change: owners, easement holders, lenders whose collateral might be impaired, city or county road authority, State of Minnesota if lakeshore is involved
Elements Burden of Proof Standard of Proof Defenses	)) Varies with underlying cause of action))
Oddities	Oral agreements and "gentlemen's agreements" that violate the Statute of Frauds are void without conduct to take the agreement out of the statute of frauds (example, partial performance)

Version 7.1   July 1, 2023

The statute covers all interests in real estate including contracts-for-deed, deeds, easements, mortgages and leases for a term exceeding one year (short-term leases can be oral agreements and still enforceable).

Special Torrens Note

If the relief sought primarily involves altering the face of a Certificate of Title (change owners, tenancy, legal description, liens), the case must be brought as a Proceeding Subsequent.

Rule 215 Minn. Gen. R. Prac. requires an order in a civil case that affects Torrens land to be approved as to form by Examiner of Titles before presentation to court.

Citations

In order to satisfy the Statute of Frauds, an agreement must:
1. be in writing, and
2. be signed by the person whose interest is to be charged

Minn. Stat. 513.05 specifically covers long-term leases and purchase agreements. To be valid, they must:
1. be in writing
2. be signed by the person whose interest is to be charged (landowner)
3. contain an adequate legal description to identify the property being sold
4. set forth the terms and conditions of the sale including purchase price.

Real Estate Reference Guide for Judges

Doyle v. Wholrabe, 66 N.W.2 757 (Minn. 1954)

A contract for the sale of land, to be enforceable, must be sufficiently definite so all the terms can be determined from the contract.
Lake Co. v. Molan, 131 N.W.2d 734 (Minn. 1964)

A contract that leaves terms to a future agreement is incomplete and unenforceable.
Scanlon v Oliver, 44 N.W. 1031 (Minn. 1890)

An oral contract can be taken out of the Statute of Frauds and Specific Performance awarded to enforce it where one party has taken possession and made payments in partial performance of the agreement.
Formanek v. Langton, 134 N.W.2d 883 (Minn. 1965)

Nathan Bissonette

Streets and Access – Overview

For title purposes, there is no difference between a street, road, alley, trail, highway, thoroughfare, cul-de-sac or expressway; they all describe an area of land over which the general public has the right to travel. For purposes of this section, they're lumped together under the general term "streets."

There is a difference between the general public having the right to cross land (a right-of-way of "street") versus one or more specific individuals having the right to cross certain lands in order to have access to certain other lands (an easement or private cartway). In this section, they're lumped together under the general term "access."

The owner of a parcel of land which abuts a street has access to the land via the street. An owner of a parcel of land which does not abut a street (remember, we're using "street" to mean "public right-of-way") does not have access to his land. That parcel is land-locked. Title to that parcel is not marketable.

The absolutely essential need to have access to land is the wellspring of endless litigation. Is there a street? How was it created? Where is it located? Is it still in existence? Did it go away? How did it go away? Was it abandoned? Has it been vacated? Who owns that land after the street goes away? If there is no street, is there a different form of access? Must access be over land – would it be sufficient if the access was by canoe over public waters? How was the right of access created, where is it located, who can use it, is it still in existence, and how do we get rid of it when we no longer need it? This might be a good area to seek an advisory opinion or appoint a Rule 53 Master.

Streets are most commonly created by dedication in a subdivision plat. A street, alley or cartway that is dedicated to the public in the plat is a public street. The procedure is well understood and rarely challenged nowadays so streets created by plat dedication are not

Real Estate Reference Guide for Judges

covered in this guide. The following sections cover the most commonly litigated topics.

Abandonment – a decision by the Court that a street no longer exists.

Cartway – a private right of access granted for the benefit of a landlocked parcel but not by the owner of the parcel burdened by the cartway; it's granted by the local government.

Implied Easement, Easement by Necessity, Prescriptive Easement – private access rights granted by the Court.

Statutory User and Common law dedication – different procedures by which public streets can be created over private land based in part on use of those lands by the public, generally without explicit consent of the owner of the burdened lands.

Vacation – the procedure the government follows to get rid of a street no longer needed.

2019 update:
Road was created by County Board Order in 1869, never recorded with the county land records. Even though not recorded, once created, the road is not subject to the Marketable Title Act (no need to continuously record renewal notices) because the existence of the road is sufficient notice of the public's rights.
County of Pope v. Kirkeby, A18-0406, unpublished (Minn. App. 2018)

2020 update:
City of Duluth had authority to issue a permit for private driveway in platted but unopened street. The purchaser of

land within a plat is entitled to use streets dedicated on the plat, even if unopened by City.
Bolen v. Glass, 755 N.W.2d 1 (Minn. 2008).

2021 update:
The dedication of a street in a plat does not convey fee title to the public but only an easement. Ownership of the land under the street does not remain in the platter but passes from the platter to subsequent owners of adjacent lots.
Carlson v. Township of Livonia, unpublished, A20-0993 (Minn. App. 2021)

2023 update:
This 1916 case was found while researching another matter. It is included because it has a helpful explanation of the court's reasoning. The plat said, "Excepting the easterly fifteen feet of said Lot A, which is reserved for a foot and bicycle path for the benefit at all times of any and all of the owners of any of the land in said East Shore Park." It was held that the word "excepting" was construed to mean "granted" to effectuate the manifest intent of the Grantor to create the easement. This case is useful when interpreting legal descriptions such as, "Lot 1 except that part taken for street." Title to a platted lot includes title to the lands under the street but by the plain language of the deed, the Grantor excepted the land under the street from the conveyance. Nobody does that. A more sensible interpretation of the deed is, "Lot 1 subject to street." The *Aldrich* case provides additional precedent for the court to construe conveyances by intent of the Grantor, not by their plain language.
Aldrich v. Soucheray, 158 N. W. 637 (Minn. 1916)

Similarly, a deed which conveyed lands extending from Marshall Street to a 12-foot alley "reserved by John Kopp" did not retain title to lands under the alley but created an easement for alley appurtenant to the platted lots. "The day is long since past for adhering to technical or literal meaning of particular words in a deed or other contract against the

plain intention of the parties as gathered from the entire instrument."
Long v. Fewer, 54 N.W. 1071 (Minn. 1893)

Second appeal on the Carlson case, above, affirms the main points. Carlsons own a platted lot. Their lot abuts an edge street. Across the street is Lake Freemont. Title to the lands under the street belong to the owners of the platted lot (Carlson) which entitled them to riparian rights in the lake including the right to place a dock. The fact the street is unimproved and designated minimum maintenance does not make it private property which they can block and does not entitle them to exclusive riparian rights as to that bit of lakeshore. Riparian rights are shared with all other riparian owners on the lake.
Carlson v. Township of Livonia, unpublished, A22-0020 (Minn. App. 2022)

Streets and Access – Abandonment

Summary	A street is an easement. The easement can be voluntarily extinguished (see Vacation, below), or it can be abandoned. Cases are generally brought to establish ownership of the land where the street formerly lay.
Statute	Minn. Stat. 541.023, Subd. 5
Limitations	None
Necessary Parties	Unit of government having authority for the street, all persons whose property will be affected by loss of the public right-of-way
Elements	The street has been abandoned
Burden of Proof	Person seeking to remove the right-of-way
Standard of Proof	Preponderance
Defenses	The street has **not** been abandoned.
Oddities	None
Special Torrens Note	Where a street is not mentioned on a Certificate of Title, an action to declare that street abandoned does not primarily seek to alter a Certificate of Title so the action need not be brought as a Proceeding Subsequent, but the resulting order will be recorded on the certificates of title for abutting lands in order to document the abandonment and, thus, Rule 215 Minn. Gen. R. Prac. requires that order to be approved as to form by Examiner of Titles before presentation to court.

Where a street is specifically mentioned on a Certificate of Title as encumbering the land |

and the relief sought is an alteration of the Certificate of Title to remove that encumbrance on the grounds that the street has been abandoned, the action must be brought as a Proceeding Subsequent.

Citations

Platted streets are easements which can be abandoned. However, more than non-use is required to establish abandonment; rather, "affirmative unequivocal acts" showing intent to abandon must be shown, e.g., placement of a "test well in the center of the platted street," placement of "telephone poles thereon in such a way as to block the free use thereof as a highway," and designation of "substitute highways."

State by Burnquist v. Marcks, 36 N.W.2d 594 (Minn. 1949)

City of Rochester v. North Side Corp., 1 N.W.2d 361 (Minn. 1941)

Parker v. City of St. Paul, 50 N.W. 247 (Minn. 1891)

Unrecorded town roads may be presumed abandoned under Subdivision 5 of the Marketable Title Act, Minn. Stat. 541.023, Subd. 5, but that presumption can be overcome by proof that the township is actually using the road.

Sterling Township v. Griffin, 244 N.W.2d 129 (Minn. 1976)

A party wanting to assert the Marketable Title Act to defeat a road must prove it has ownership in fee simple title. The road authority can adduce evidence that a road has been established by Statutory User. The case turns on the facts.

Town of Belle Prairie v. Kilber, 448 N.W. 2d 375 (Minn. App. 1989)

A municipality can be estopped from asserting the street has not been abandoned only when all the following elements are present:
1. long-continued nonuse by the municipality
2. possession by a private party in good faith and in the belief the street was abandoned
3. erection of valuable improvements on the property without city objection
4. great damage to the possessor if the city reclaimed the street
5. an unequivocal act by the city which, in light of all the circumstances, induced a third party reasonably to believe the street was abandoned.

Reads Landing Campers Association v. Township of Pepin, 533 N.W.2d 45 (Minn. App. 1995) (found street had not been abandoned); affirmed 546 N.W.2d 10 (Minn. 1996) (there were not enough unequivocal acts to prove abandonment of streets).

Real Estate Reference Guide for Judges

Streets and Access - Cartway

Summary	A cartway is a statutory means of obtaining access to "landlocked" real property. A cartway is generally a public roadway.
Statute	Minn. Stat. 164.08 (authority to establish cartway over land located in township or county), Minn. Stat. 435.37 (authority to establish cartway over land located in city), Minn. Stat. 164.07 (procedure to use in establishing any cartway, wherever located)
Limitations	No applicable limitations period for filing of cartway petition. On appeal to district court, if cartway was granted by town/county/city, appeal must be filed within 40 days from the filing of the award of damages with the town/county/city's clerk and within 10 days in order to delay opening of cartway. If cartway is rejected by town/county/city, appeal must be filed within 1 year from the filing of the order with the town/county/city's clerk.
Necessary Parties	Affected landowners, interested parties and occupants. Minn. Stat. 164.07.
Elements	*Permissive establishment:* under Minn. Stat. 164.08, Subd. 1 (town/county only), town/county may establish cartway 2 rods (33 feet) wide and not more than ½ mile long upon petition presented to the board signed by at least 5 voters, landowners of the town,

requesting cartway on a section line to serve tract(s) of land consisting of at least 150 acres, at least 100 acres of which are tillable.

Mandatory establishment: under Minn. Stat. 164.08, Subd. 2 (town/county) or Minn. Stat. 435.37, Subd. 1 (city), the board/council shall establish a cartway if the petitioner is: (1) the owner of a tract of land containing at least 5 acres*; (2) who has no access thereto except over a navigable waterway or over the land of others; or (3) whose access is less than 2 rods (33 ft) in width.

> *It is also possible for an owner of a parcel containing at least 2 but less than 5 acres to acquire cartway, if parcel was of record as separate parcel as of January 1, 1998 and if land has no access thereto except over a navigable waterway or over lands of others.

The cartway must connect the petitioner's land with a public road.

> Note: acreage requirement can be met by totaling the acreage of petitioners for separate parcels to be served by the cartway.

> Damages. If cartway is granted, petitioner must pay damages to affected landowners for the taking. Damages are generally measured by estimating value of the land taken as well as severance damages (the difference in market value immediately before the taking and the market value of the remaining tract

after the taking). Also to be determined for damages is the money value of the benefits which establishment of the cartway will confer on the affected landowner and deduct the benefits, if any, from the damages, if any, and award the difference, if any, as damages (e.g. if an affected landowner is also landlocked and secures access to his or her own property via the cartway petition of another landowner, this is a benefit to the "affected" landowner as well as the petitioner).

Burden of Proof	Minn. Stat. 164.07 provides that an appeal from the establishment or denial of a cartway is tried in the same manner as eminent domain (condemnation) proceedings under Minn. Stat. Chapter 117. The burden of proof is on the appealing party.
Standard of Proof	Town/county/city that grants or refuses a cartway acts in a legislative capacity and will be reversed on appeal only when: (1) the evidence is clearly against the decision; (2) an erroneous theory of law was applied; or (3) the board acted arbitrarily and capriciously, contrary to the public's best interest.
Defenses	If petitioner meets all statutory requirements, establishment is mandatory. However, town/county/city may exercise reasonable discretion in varying the route proposed if it determines both that an alternative route will be less disruptive and damaging to neighbors and that the alternative route is in the public's best interest.

Oddities	There is dispute among practitioners about the effect of a private interest lying between the petitioner's land and the public road. For example, assume cartway crosses one parcel, then petitioner has an easement over next parcel. Does that mean the cartway fails to connect the petitioner's land to a public road because the public does not have the right to use the private easement?
	Definition of "landlocked" can be ambiguous. A landowner is landlocked for purposes of the statute if existing access is not "meaningful" (e.g. leads to an unusable or topographically impossible location), is by water only, or is less than 33 feet.
	Minn. Stat. 164.07 does not state that the owners of the land must be served; the statute only expressly requires that "occupants" of the land be served with notice of the cartway hearing.
Special Torrens Note	Torrens property is not exempt from the imposition of a cartway. The case does not seek to change title shown on the Certificate of Title, so it need not be brought as a Proceeding Subsequent.
	Rule 215 Minn. Gen. R. Prac. requires an order in a civil case that affects Torrens property to be approved as to form by the Examiner of Titles before presentation to the court.

Real Estate Reference Guide for Judges

Citations

> Multiple owners of tracts totaling at least 5 acres may join together in a petition for a cartway.
> *Watson v. Board of Supervisors of Town of South Side*, 239 N.W. 913 (Minn. 1931)

> Establishment of a cartway is mandatory if the petitioner meets the statutory requirements.
> *Roemer v. Board of Supervisors of Elysian Twp.*, 167 N.W.2d 497 (1969)

> Landowners are entitled to a cartway if existing access leads to an unusable or topographically impossible location.
> *Kennedy v. Pepin Tp. of Wabasha County*, 784 N.W.2d 378 (Minn. 2010)

> Having access to the land by water does not rule out a cartway.
> *In re Daniel for Establishment of Cartway*, 644 N.W.2d 495 (Minn. App. 2002) (town board, county board, trial court and Court of Appeals held that if you only have access to your land over water, that's not good enough so you are entitled to a cartway over lands of your neighbors. The Supreme Court reversed at 656 N.W.2d 543 (Minn. 2003), saying access by canoe was good enough, no cartway was needed. The legislature responded in 2004 by amending Minn. Stat. 164.08, Subd. 2(a) to clarify that access to land by a navigable waterway did not prevent the landowner from receiving a cartway.

> A landowner is not required to exhaust other viable legal remedies that might provide access prior to pursuing a cartway.
> *In re Daniels for Establishment of a Cartway in Glenwood Township.*, A06-571 unpublished (Minn. App. 2007)

Establishment of a cartway is an exercise of eminent domain, the inherent power of a governmental entity to take privately owned property and convert it to public use, provided the owner is compensated.
> *Powell v. Town Bd. of Sinnott Twp.,* 221 N.W. 527 (Minn. 1928)
> *Mueller v. Supervisors of Town of Courtland,* 135 N.W. 996 (Minn. 1912)
> *Silver v. Ridgeway,* 733 N.W.2d 165 (Minn. App. 2007)

A town board acts in its legislative capacity when establishing a cartway and its action will be set aside by the district court only when: (i) the evidence is practically conclusive against it; (ii) the board proceeded on an erroneous theory of law; or (iii) the board acted arbitrarily and capriciously, contrary to the public's best interest.
> *Rask v. Town Board of Hendrum,* 218 N.W.115 (Minn. 1928)

A cartway is a form of condemnation/eminent domain. Proceedings are administered by:
- (i) town board when land located within a township (Minn. Stat. 164.08);
- (ii) county board when land located in unorganized territory (Minn. Stat. 164.08, Subd. 2(b));
- (iii) city council when land located within city (Minn. Stat. 435.37).

Appellate procedure is governed by Minn. Stat. 164.07 regardless of whether land is located in town/county/city. Appeal is to district court under Minn. Stat. 164.07, Subd. 7.

Real Estate Reference Guide for Judges

Notice of Appeal must be filed with district court administrator of county where lands lie within 40 days after filing of award of damages with town/county/city clerk.

Public purpose/necessity of cartway and damages can be appealed. Although not expressly stated Minn. Stat. 164.07, it is generally accepted that cartway location/route can also be appealed.

Notice of Appeal must include bond of not less than $250. Minn. Stat. 164.07, Subd. 7. Older cases imply the trial court is without jurisdiction to hear the appeal if a bond is not posted, but a recent unpublished opinion distinguishes those cases and holds the lack of a bond does not deprive the trial court of jurisdiction to hear an appeal in a cartway case.
In re Petition of Hanlon, A09-1563 unpublished (Minn. App. 2010)

Appellant must mail a copy of the Notice of Appeal by registered or certified mail to the clerk or any board member of the town/county/city.

Appeal is entered upon the calendar for trial at the next general term of court occurring more than 20 days after appeal is perfected and is tried in the same manner as appeal in eminent domain proceedings under Chapter 117 of the Minnesota Statutes. Minn. Stat. 164.07, Subd. 8.

On appeal, damages are decided de novo by a jury.

Order should include Findings of Fact and Conclusions of Law concerning whether the evidence is clearly against the town/county/city's decision, whether an erroneous theory of law was applied, and whether the town/county/city acted arbitrarily and capriciously, contrary to the public's best interest.

Nathan Bissonette

2018 update:
Cartway was established in 2006, Zuckerman was ordered to pay damages to Ratfield but didn't, Ratfield's 2016 action for damages was barred by the six-year statute of limitations in Minn. Stat. 541.05, Subd. 1(4).
Ratfield v. Zuckerman, unpublished, A17-0214 (Minn. App. 2017)

2019 update:
Township award of cartway upheld. Standard of review explained.
Cich v. Bay Lake Township, unpublished, A18-0542 (Minn. App. 2018)

2022 update:
A Town Board cannot grant a cartway where legally enforceable access to a public road already exists but the question of whether that access is "meaningful access" is a determination for the Board. The Board's establishment of a cartway was supported by evidence and was not arbitrary, capricious, or an error of law. The district court erred by substituting its judgment for that of the Board. Reversed.
Idyllwood Homeowners Association v. Town of Ideal, unpublished, A21-0903 (Minn. App. 2022)

2023 update:
The Town Board can grant a cartway to Petitioner and award damages to the landowner whose lands the cartway will cross (the burdened landowner). The proper measure of damages in this case was the "before and after" rule, comparing the fair market value of the burdened landowner's property before and after the cartway. The value of any existing improvements damaged by the cartway may be factored into the damages calculation only to the extent that it impacts the fair market value of the property, not as a separate measure of additional damages.
Heggemeyer v. Spalding Township, unpublished, A22-0805 (Minn. App. 2023)

Real Estate Reference Guide for Judges

A parcel served by an existing 'state forest road' over DNR lands is landlocked under the language of the statute and therefore is entitled to a cartway. Town board was not required to consider, much less select, an alternative route.
In re Wartman, unpublished, A22-0450, (Minn. App. 2022)

Streets and Access – Implied Easements and Easements by Necessity

Summary	Implied easements are often sought when land is landlocked. The basis is that a party failed to include a necessary easement in the conveyance.
	Courts have often treated the terms "implied easement" and "easement by necessity" interchangeably.
Statute	Usually pled as Declaratory Judgment under Chapter 555 or Action to Determine Adverse Claims under Chapter 559.
Limitations	No applicable limitations period.
Necessary Parties	Landowners of record, lien holders, occupants, encroachers, persons know to Plaintiff to have a claim or interest that does not appear of record.
Elements	When a landowner conveys a portion of land that has no access, the owner of the purchased portion has a right of access across the retained lands of the grantor unless the conveying document explicitly disclaims any right of access.
	Essential elements of an implied easement are: (i) unity of title; (ii) separation of title; (iii) the use which gives rise to the easement shall have been so long continued and apparent as

Real Estate Reference Guide for Judges

to show that it was intended to be permanent; and (iv) the easement is necessary to the benefit enjoyment of the land granted.

Burden of Proof	Party asserting easement.
Standard of Proof	Preponderance of the evidence (no articulated standard).
Defenses	Except for necessity requirement, elements are only aids in determining whether implied easement exists.
Oddities	To be "necessary," easement must be more than mere convenience but need not be indispensable; a reasonable necessity is sufficient.
	Entitlement to easement is determined at time of title severance. Subsequent change of conditions does not defeat an implied easement if one was created upon severance.
	Topography, structures, vegetation, zoning ordinances or the need for extensive paving may create conditions where an easement is implied by necessity.
	This is an equitable doctrine, so courts examine the equities.
Special Torrens Note	Case law has not addressed the question of whether an implied easement can encumber Torrens property. Minn. Stat. 508.02 says

registration of land does not operate to change or affect any rights, burdens, liabilities, or obligations created by law and applicable to unregistered land except as otherwise expressly provided in Chapter 508. Chapter 508 does not expressly prohibit an implied easement over Torrens land.

An action to establish an implied easement seeks to change the rights shown on the face of the Certificate of Title; therefore, it should be brought as a Proceeding Subsequent.

Rule 215 Minn. Gen. R. Prac. requires an order in a civil case that affects Torrens land to be approved as to form by Examiner of Titles before presentation to court.

Citations

The terms "easement by necessity" and "easement by implication" are interchangeable.
Bode v. Bode, 494 N.W.2d 301, 304 n.1 (Minn. App. 1992).

Essential elements of "implied easement": (i) unity of title; (ii) a separation of title; (iii) the use which gives rise to the easement shall have been so long continued and apparent as to show that it was intended to be permanent; and (iv) the easement is necessary to the beneficial enjoyment of the land granted.
Clark v. Galaxy Apartments, 427 N.W.2d 723 (Minn. App. 1988)

While an easement will not be implied unless it is necessary, all three elements are used as indicia of the parties' intent to create an easement.

Real Estate Reference Guide for Judges

Lake George Park, L.L.C. v. IBM Mid America Employees Federal Credit Union, 576 N.W.2d 463 (Minn. App.1998), citing *Olson v. Mullen*, 68 N.W.2d 640 (Minn. 1955)

An easement is implied when: (1) there was separation of title; (2) use of the easement was so long continued and apparent as to show that it was intended to be permanent; and (3) the easement is necessary to the beneficial enjoyment of the land.
    Magnuson v. Cossette, 707 N.W.2d 738 (Minn. App. 2006)
    Romanchuk v. Plotkin, 9 N.W.2d 421 (Minn. 1943)
    Rosendahl v. Nelson, 408 N.W.2d 609 (Minn. App. 1987)

The necessity factor is the only requirement while the other two factors "are only aids" in the analysis.
    Rosendahl, supra, (citing *Olson v. Mullen*, 68 N.W.2d 640 (Minn. 1955)

The existence of an implied easement is determined at the time of separation.
    Lake George Park, L.L.C. v. IBM Mid America Employees Federal Credit Union, 576 N.W.2d 463 (Minn. App.1998)

"Necessary" means more than a mere convenience. However, the easement need not be indispensable to be necessary; rather, a reasonable necessity is sufficient.
    Clark v. Galaxy Apartments, 427 N.W.2d 723 (Minn. App. 1988)

Entitlement to implied easement is determined at the time of severance, and a subsequent change of conditions will not defeat or create an implied easement."

Clark v. Galaxy Apartments, 427 N.W.2d 723 (Minn. App. 1988)

Obstacles such as topography, houses, trees, zoning ordinances, or the need for extensive paving may create conditions when an easement is implied by necessity.
    Rosendahl v. Nelson, 408 N.W.2d 609 (Minn. App. 1987)

An easement by necessity lasts only as long as the necessity. Necessity for the easement is eliminated when the owner of the dominant estate acquires a permanent legal right to public access to the estate.
    Bode v. Bode, 494 N.W.2d 301 (Minn. App. 1992)

The topography of Appellant's land made a driveway in the desired location expensive but as there were other areas on Appellant's land where a driveway could be constructed that would adequately serve the property, Appellant could not establish an easement by necessity over the neighbor's land. Appellant could not satisfy the elements of an easement by prescription and could not show a mutual mistake in the vesting deed to justify reforming the deed to include an easement.
    Wilderness Resort Villas, LLC v. Miller, unpublished, A07-0557 (Minn. App. 2008)

Order should include:
    Findings of Fact regarding the elements of an implied easement.
    Conclusion of Law stating a preponderance of the evidence.
    The legal descriptions of the easement and affected properties.

Real Estate Reference Guide for Judges

2018 update:
Street automatically includes utility easements.
>Carter v. Nw. Tel. Exch. Co., 63 N.W. 111 (Minn. 1895)
>Minneapolis Gas Co. v. Zimmerman, 91 N.W.2d 642 (Minn. 1958)

2023 update:
Developer split a large lot into two smaller lots, A (which had access to a public right of way) and B (which was landlocked). An access easement across A for the benefit of B was not recorded. 15 years later, Developer sought an easement by necessity over A for the benefit of B. Held: The easement over A was necessary to the beneficial enjoyment of B, but Developer's claim is barred by laches and unclean hands. Lot B remains landlocked and undeveloped.
>In re Bacchus, unpublished, A22-0610 (Minn. App. 2023)

Easement by necessity existed when lands were split, despite nearby platted road which was never built due to difficult land conditions including a steep hill and wetlands.
>Olson v. Jackson, unpublished, A22-0739 (Minn. App. 2023)

Streets and Access – Prescriptive Easements

Summary	A prescriptive easement is based on prior continuous use and grants a right to use the property of another. It does not carry with it title or a right of possession in the land itself.
Statute	Usually pled as Declaratory Judgment under chapter 555 or Action to Determine Adverse Claims under Chapter 559.
Limitations	Minn. Stat. 541.02 – cannot bring the claim until 15 years have passed.
Necessary Parties	Landowners of record, lien holders, occupants, encroachers, persons known to Plaintiff to have a claim or interest that does not appear of record.
Elements	The elements of a prescriptive easement are generally the same as those necessary to establish adverse possession: hostile, actual, open, continuous and exclusive use for 15 years. The scope of a prescriptive easement can be very limited (e.g. May to October only), as it is measured and defined by the use made of the land giving rise to the easement.
Burden of Proof	Person seeking to establish right to use. Once elements are proved by person seeking to establish right to use, burden shifts to owner of land over which claimed easement

Real Estate Reference Guide for Judges

	crosses. Owner of land must then prove that use was permissive.
Standard of Proof	**Clear and convincing,** in general.
Defenses	Must prove all elements; failure on any is fatal.
Oddities	Claimant can "tack" a prior owner's time of use to claimant's time of use to meet the 15-year requirement if there is privity between owners.
	In rural or undeveloped areas, occasional or sporadic use can give rise to a prescriptive easement.
	There is a rebuttable presumption that use is permissive if the claimed easement crosses land owned by a relative of the claimant.
	A prescriptive easement cannot be established over property owned by a governmental unit or over one's own land.
Special Torrens Note	A prescriptive easement cannot be established over Torrens property. Minn. Stat. 508.02.

Citations
Clear and convincing evidence of actual, open, hostile, continuous, and exclusive use for 15 years.
McCuen v. McCarvel, 263 N.W.2d 64 (Minn. 1978)
Rogers v. Moore, 603 N.W.2d 650 (Minn. 1999)

Actual and open possession requires unconcealed, visible possessory acts upon the land such that the owner might be apprised that another is claiming rights in the land.
    Hickerson v. Bender, 500 N.W.2d 169 (Minn. App. 1993)

In prescriptive easements, the scope of the easement is defined by the actual use.
    Block v. Sexton, 577 N.W.2d 521 (Minn. App. 1998)

Evidence of use of a driveway is highly persuasive evidence of the existence of a driveway easement and prior use of it.
    Rogers v. Moore, 603 N.W.2d 650 (Minn. 1999)
    Nordin v. Kuno, 287 N.W.2d 923 (Minn. 1980)
    In the Matter of Mehrkens v. Ryan, C7-03-15, unpublished (Minn. App. 2003)

Exclusivity, for purposes of obtaining a prescriptive easement, does not require a claimant to have excluded use by others. Use is "exclusive" when it does not "depend on a similar right in others," and is "exclusive against the community at large."
    Merrick v. Schleuder, 228 N.W. 755 (Minn. 1930)
    Wheeler v. Newman, 394 N.W.2d 620 (Minn. App. 1986)

Successive use can be tacked to total 15 years if there is privity between users.
    Fredericksen v. Henke, 209 N.W. 257 (Minn. 1926)

In rural or undeveloped areas, occasional and sporadic use may give rise to a prescriptive easement.
    Skala v. Lindbeck, 214 N.W. 271 (Minn. 1927)

Scope of prescriptive easement is measured and defined by use giving rise to the easement. "This . . . does not mean that

Real Estate Reference Guide for Judges

the right can be acquired by occasional and sporadic acts for temporary purposes."
> *Romans v. Nadler*, 14 N.W.2d 482, 485 (Minn. 1944)

Once a prescriptive easement is established, it becomes an absolute right unaffected by later breaks in use.
> *Dozier v. Krmpotich*, 35 N.W.2d 696 (Minn. 1949)

A prescriptive easement can be very limited, such as limiting the right to use to the months of May through October based on historical use.
> *Block v. Sexton*, 577 N.W.2d 521 (Minn. App. 1998)

Once a prescriptive easement comes into existence, it passes to subsequent owners.
> *Swedish-American Nat'l Bank of Minneapolis v. Connecticut Mutual Life Insurance Co.*, 86 N.W. 420 (Minn. 1901)

Holder is not limited to particular method of use in vogue when the easement was acquired; other methods of use in the aid of the general purpose for which the easement was acquired are permissible.
> *Washington Wildlife Preservation, Inc. v. State*, 329 N.W.2d 543 (Minn. 1983)

Claimant cannot acquire a prescriptive easement over public land.
> *Heuer v. County of Aitkin*, 645 N.W.2d 753 (Minn. App. 2002)

In prescriptive easement cases, if the claimant can prove all of the other elements clearly, then the claimant will have the benefit of the doubt on the original entry being hostile, i.e., without consent.
> *Nordin v. Kuno*, 287 N.W.2d 923 (Minn. 1980)

This presumption can be rebutted if the disseized owner has evidence that demonstrates that the original entry was permissive. In effect, once the other elements are shown, the burden of proof regarding hostility shifts to the defendant.
Boldt v. Roth, 618 N.W.2d 393 (Minn. 2000)

The meaning of the term "exclusive use" also differs; of course, multiple parties can make use of the same easement.

"Minnesota law is clear, however, that exclusivity for a prescriptive easement is not as strictly construed as for adverse possession . . . The use need not be exclusive in the sense that it must be used by one person only . . . Rather, the right must not depend upon a similar right in others; it must be exclusive against the community at large."
Nordin v. Kuno, 287 N.W.2d 923, 926 (Minn. 1980)

Order should include:
    Findings of Fact reciting the evidence for each factor including length of time of use.
    Conclusion of Law stating evidence was clear and convincing.
    The legal description of the lands owned by the acquiring party including the newly acquired easement.

Streets and Access – Statutory User and Common Law Dedication

Summary	Statutory user provides for establishment of a public roadway if the roadway has been used and repaired in a certain manner.
	Common law dedication, which is based upon contract theory, can also give rise to access rights. Under this theory, a landowner "intends" for the public to use the land as a road.
Statute	Statutory user: Minn. Stat. 160.05
	Common law dedication is not statutory.
Limitations	Statutory user: at least 6 continuous years of use and maintenance must precede claim.
	Common law dedication: no applicable limitations period.
Necessary Parties	Landowners, claimants, lien holders, occupants, encroachers, persons known to Plaintiff to have a claim or interest that does not appear of record.
Elements	Statutory user: when any road or portion of a road has been used and kept in repair and worked for at least six years continuously as a public highway by a road authority, it shall be deemed dedicated to the public to the width of the actual use and be and remain, until

lawfully vacated, a public highway whether it has ever been established as a public highway or not.

Common law dedication: the owner's intention for the road to be used as a public road equates to an "offer," while the public's use of the road OR the road authority's maintenance of the road acts as the public's "acceptance." Intent can be implied or express.

Burden of Proof	Party seeking to establish roadway.
Standard of Proof	Preponderance of the evidence.
Defenses	Statutory user: failure to meet 6 years, failure to meet continuity requirement, private maintenance instead of maintenance by road authority, no public use.
	Common law dedication: lack of intent, private maintenance instead of maintenance by road authority, no public use.
	Dedication, whether statutory or common law, conveys only the estate necessary to fulfill the purposes of the dedication.
	An easement can be lost by abandonment.
Oddities	Statutory user is similar to a prescriptive easement claim, although the required time period is shorter (6 years versus 15 years) and the result is a public roadway instead of a private easement.

Real Estate Reference Guide for Judges

Either use or maintenance is sufficient to establish that a common law dedication has occurred.

Special Torrens Note — Neither statutory user dedication nor common law dedication apply to Torrens land.

Citations

Standard of proof to establish statutory dedication of a road is a preponderance of the evidence (expressly over-ruling clear and convincing standard in *Foster v. Bergstrom,* 515 N.W.2d 581 (Minn. App. 1994)).
Rixmann v. City of Prior Lake, 723 N.W.2d 493 (Minn. App. 2006)

To prove common law dedication, one must show the property owner's express or implied consent to devote the land to public use and the public's acceptance of that use.
Wojahn v. Johnson, 297 N.W.2d 298 (Minn. 1980)
Sackett v. Storm, 480 N.W.2d 377 (Minn. App. 1992), *review denied* (March 26, 1992)

Intent to dedicate need not be a conscious intent but may be inferred from owner's unequivocal conduct.
Anderson v. Birkeland, 38 N.W.2d 215 (Minn. 1949)

Whether owner intended to dedicate land and whether the public accepted the dedication are questions of fact.
Keiter v. Berge, 18 N.W.2d 35 (Minn. 1945)

Once public accepts owner's dedication, it is immediately effective.
Daugherty v. Sowers, 68 N.W.2d 866 (Minn. 1955)

Dedication is irrevocable after public acceptance unless public consents to revocation.
    Keiter v. Berge, 18 N.W.2d 35 (Minn. 1945)

Owner's dedication binds his or her successors.
    Daugherty v. Sowers, 68 N.W.2d 866 (Minn. 1955)

The width of a road established by common law dedication is the actual width of use, including roadway, slopes, ditches and where appropriate, stores, turnaround or lay-by.
    Township of Villard v. Hoting, 442 N.W.2d 826 (Minn. App. 1989)

To satisfy the maintenance requirement, the maintenance must be of a quality and character appropriate to an already existing public road.
    Town of Belle Prairie v. Kilber, 448 N.W.2d 375 (Minn. App. 1989)

To meet the statutory maintenance requirement, it is sufficient if maintenance is performed when necessary.
    Hansen v. Town of Verdi, 85 N.W. 906 (Minn. 1901)
    Northfork Twp. v. Joffer, 353 N.W.2d 216 (Minn. App. 1984)

Statutory dedication under Minn. Stat. 160.05 is a form of adverse possession prohibited by the Torrens Act.
    Hebert v. City of Fifty Lakes, 784 N.W.2d 848 (Minn. App. 2010)

Common law dedication based on an implied intent to dedicate is prohibited under the Torrens Act.
    Hebert v. City of Fifty Lakes, 784 N.W.2d 848 (Minn. App. 2010)

Real Estate Reference Guide for Judges

Order should include:
>Findings of Fact regarding use and maintenance.
>For statutory user claim, Finding of Fact regarding period of use.
>For common law dedication claim, Finding of Fact regarding intent of owner.
>Conclusion of Law stating preponderance of the evidence.
>The legal descriptions of the claimed roadway and the affected property.

2023 update:
>A town road may become a 'public road' through common law dedication by use, but that does not force the Town Board to assume maintenance. The Town can determine when and if to accept the road.
>>*Zimmer v. Pine Lake Township*, (citation pending), A22-1606 (Minn. App. 2023)

Streets and Access – Vacation

Summary	When a street is lawfully vacated, the easement granting the public the right to travel the street ceases to exist, and the title to the land under the street reverts to the underlying fee owners of the property for their exclusive use and enjoyment.

Note that the terms street, road, alley, highway and right-of-way are often used interchangeably, and there is no legal difference. |
Statute	The applicable statute varies based upon the location of the street, whether it is platted or un-platted, and whether the proceeding is through the city, town, county or the district court.
Limitations	No applicable limitations period.
Necessary Parties	All persons owning or occupying land that would be affected by the proposed vacation, which generally includes all owners and occupants within the plat and the Commissioner of Natural Resources IF any part of street terminates at, abuts upon, or is adjacent to any public water.
Elements	Varies by governing statute:

Minn. Stat. 164.07: vacation of platted or un-platted streets within township or county.

Minn. Stat. 412.851: vacation of statutory city streets. |

Real Estate Reference Guide for Judges

Minn. Stat. 410.33: vacation of streets in home rule charter cities.

Minn. Stat. 440.13: vacation of streets in fourth class home rule charter cities.

Minn. Stat. 440.135: vacation of streets in third class charter cities.

Minn. Stat. 505.14: vacation of platted roads by district court.

Burden of Proof	Party seeking vacation
Standard of Proof	Preponderance of the evidence **(see 2018 Update)**
Defenses	Party seeking vacation did not meet standard of proof.
Oddities	A person seeking vacation of a platted street may use either the provisions discussed previously for a petition to the municipality or court for a vacation or may choose to apply directly to the district court for a vacation. Petitioners are not required to first petition a municipality or county for the vacation before approaching the courts.

The law presumes property owners along the vacated street each "contributed" land up to the center of the street. As a result, upon vacation, title to half of the street usually reverts to each abutting property owner. This rule does not apply where evidence shows the street was laid out wholly on one of the abutting owner's land (e.g. if the road is on the edge of a plat). In this instance, the landowner contributing all of the land obtains title to the entire portion of the vacated roadway abutting his land unless the same owner owned both sides of the street; in that case, the court must determine if he intended the street to serve the other lands.

Special Torrens Note

In many counties, the owner of vacated land must petition the Examiner of Titles to add the fee interest to the face of the Certificate of Title (instead of carrying the vacation as a memorial). Also, subsequent conveyances must reference the vacated street or it will not be included in the conveyance.

An action to vacate a street by court order under Minn. Stat. 505.14 does not primarily seek to alter a Certificate of Title, so it need not be brought as a Proceeding Subsequent, but the resulting order probably will be recorded on the certificates of title for abutting lands to document the street vacation.

Rule 215 Minn. Gen. R. Prac. requires an order in a civil case that affects Torrens land to be approved as to form by Examiner of Titles before presentation to court.

Citations

District courts have statutory authority to vacate all or part of platted city streets.
In re Verbick, 607 N.W.2d 148 (Minn. App. 2000)

The statutory procedure for street vacation under Minn. Stat. 505.14 requires service on owners or occupants of land within the platted area.

Real Estate Reference Guide for Judges

Batinich v. Harvey, 277 N.W.2d 355 (Minn. 1979)

That requirement has been softened by case-law: "We acknowledge Eye's argument that a plat "could" consist of 1,000 lots owned by 1,000 different landowners. In that case, it may stretch the bounds of reason to conclude that each and every landowner within the plat is affected by a proposal to vacate a small part of one street. But that is a case for another day. On the particular facts here, with 31 landowners owning lots close together in a small town, we are bound to apply the reasoning in *Etzler* and *Batinich*. The law requires Eye to mail notice to all landowners within the plat and because he only mailed notice to 11 of the 31 landowners, we agree with the district court that Eye failed to give proper notice as required by section 505.14."
In re Petition to Vacate Portions of Streets in Plat of Pottstown v. City of Wahkon, A04-1233 unpublished (Minn. App. 2005)

Failure to show uselessness is dispositive, requiring denial of petition.
In re Verbick, 607 N.W.2d 148 (Minn. App. 2000)

Party seeking vacation bears burden of proving street's uselessness.
In re Verbick, 607 N.W.2d 148 (Minn. App. 2000)

"Useless" should not be given restricted meaning, but rather should be ascribed its well-accepted definition, which is not serving or not capable of serving any valuable purpose,

unserviceable, producing no good end, or answering no desired purpose.
> *In re Verbick*, 607 N.W.2d 148 (Minn. App. 2000)

Lack of present use is insufficient to show uselessness required for vacation because the future may hold a greater need for use of the street than now exists.
> *In re Verbick*, 607 N.W.2d 148 (Minn. App. 2000)

Where it is proposed to vacate a street which is located upon a lake shore, the final test is whether the public interest will be best served by discontinuing the way.
> *Application of Baldwin*, 15 N.W.2d 184 (Minn. 1944)

Whether to vacate rests in sound discretion of district court.
> *In re Jamieson*, 130 N.W. 1000 (Minn. 1911)

Where street leading to boat landing had not been used by anyone in the community for almost 25 years, and town did nothing toward keeping it in repair, but street still afforded public means of access to lake, street could not be vacated.
> *Petition of Krebs*, 6 N.W.2d 803 (Minn. 1942)

"Public" includes persons other than those in immediate vicinity of street sought to be vacated, and means the "general public" which has a true concern in recreational facilities offered by lakes and means of access thereto.
> *Petition of Krebs*, 6 N.W.2d 803 (Minn. 1942)

Upon vacation, title to streets dedicated in a plat revert to the successors-in-interest of the Grantor, unless the Grantor showed an alternative intention.
> *White v. Jefferson*, 124 N.W. 373 (Minn. 1910)

Real Estate Reference Guide for Judges

Edge Streets in Plats are a problem and are treated differently from streets in the interior of the plat. See diagram below:

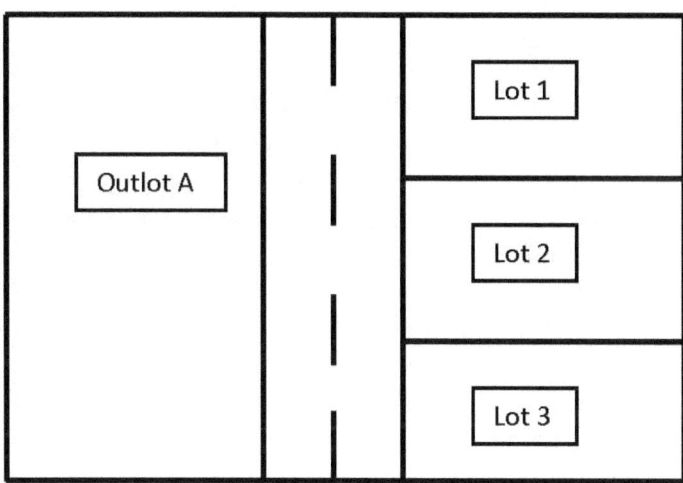

If the Developer owns the land on both sides of the street and plans to use it for the benefit of Lots 1, 2 and 3 in the Phase I of the development, and also intends to use it for the lots that eventually will be platted over Outlot A when the Developer builds Phase II of the project, then the street is treated as an interior street rather than an edge street even though all the land for the street came out of the Phase I portion of the development. When the street is vacated, ownership of the land where the street used to be, is split down the middle.

> The rebuttable presumption is that the deed to land abutting a roadway is that the deed conveys up to the center line of the street. When a different intention is manifested, or where there is no foundation for it, then the presumption is not applicable.
>
> *In Re Robbins,* 24 N.W 356 (Minn. 1885)

Nathan Bissonette

Examples of where there is no foundation for the presumption:

1. When the street is laid upon land not owned by the grantor, subsequent grantees do not obtain rights in the street.

2. Alternatively, when the street is laid upon land that is entirely owned by grantor and the land abutting the property is owned by a stranger, then the rights to subsequent grantees extend all the way to the boundary line.

    a. Unless, the grantor explicitly reserves the rights in the street to himself or another party. *White v. Jefferson*, 124 N.W. 373 (Minn. 1910)

Absent any language in the deed or conveyance, the presumption is that subsequent purchasers of land abutting a street take title to the middle of the street.

Where a street is dedicated by plat and there are lots on both sides of the street owned by the platter and dedicator, the lots on each side of the street carry title to the underlying fee only to the center of the street . . . . But, where there are lots or land owned by the dedicator on only one side of the street and he owns the lots or land only up to and including the street, so that the street extends to the boundary of his land and he owns nothing on the other side thereof, the rule seems to be that the dedicator, after parting with the lots bordering the street, retains no further fee or interest in the street, and, upon vacation thereof, the fee to the street reverts to the lot owners who obtained title from the platter or dedicator.

Lamprey v. Amer. Hoist & Derrick Co., 266 N.W. 434 Minn. 1936)

Upon vacation of street or alley, owners of land abutting street or alley own to middle of street or alley. Exception where grantor of easement owned land up to and including street, but not land on other side of street. In that case, upon vacation, fee reverts to grantees who obtain their title from grantor of easement.

> *Edgewater Cottage Association, Inc. v. Watson,* 387 N.W.2d 216 (Minn. App. 1986)

Absent an express reservation or conveyance of fee title to a dedicated road, the only situation in which an abutting owner takes title to the entire road is when the dedicator did not own the land on both sides of the road.

> *Robert Thueringer vs. Michael L. Kittridge,* A09-1046 unpublished, (Minn. App. 2010)

When allocating title to an edge street, you must examine title to the land across the street to determine whether the same owner owned both parcels at the time of platting and if so, you must determine that developer's intent for the street.

Order should include:
Finding of Fact regarding uselessness of vacated street.
Conclusion of law regarding preponderance of the evidence.
Legal descriptions for the vacated portion of street and the adjacent properties that gain fee title to the vacated street. If edge street, findings should explain who gets it and why.

2018 update:
Interested persons can petition cities, townships and counties to vacate public rights-of-way. The authority, procedures, and legal standard for vacation vary by statute and charter. The District Court sees these cases on appeal from the local government's decision and should require the government's attorney to brief the court on the procedures and standards the local government was required to follow to vacate the right-of-way, and also the standard of review the

District Court should apply when reviewing the local government's decision.

> The District Court may be asked to vacate a right-of-way itself, under Minn. Stat. 505.14. The person seeking the vacation must prove by a preponderance that the street is useless for the purpose for which it was laid out.
> *In the Matter of the Petition of Verbick to Vacate*, 607 N.W.2d, 148 (Minn. App. 2000).

2021 update:
> A town road can be vacated by the district court under Minn. Stat. 505.14, but that is not the exclusive method to vacate a town road. The town board has authority to vacate a town road under Minn. Stat. 164.07. It does not matter whether the town road was dedicated in a plat or obtained by other means. After vacation of the township's easement, ownership of the lands underlying the town road remain in the adjacent owners, but vacation does not expand the area they own. Ordinarily, title to land under a vacated interior street of a plat is presumed to run to the centerline of the street, but that rule is only presumptive and can be rebutted by a showing that the conveyance to the adjacent owner expressed a contrary intention. In this case, one owner's deed ran to "the westerly line of a dedicated public road" and "along the northerly line of said dedicated public road." Since the deed did not convey title to the centerline of the road, the vacation of the township's easement did not extend title to the center of the road.
> *Smeby v. Hanson*, unpublished, A20-1329 (Minn. App. 2021)

Tenancy

Summary	Not a separate cause of action, issue generally arises in an action for Reformation of a Document that fails to correctly state the parties' intent.
Statute	Minn. Stat. 500.19
Limitations	None; may be litigated at any time
Necessary Parties	Persons whose interests would be affected by the change, typically other owners and heirs who would be divested or dis-inherited by the change.
Elements	)
Burden of Proof	) See: Reformation of a Document, above.
Standard of Proof	)
Defenses	)
Oddities	When more than one person owns land, "tenancy" tells us what happens to the owners' shares when they die, subject to exceptions for a surviving spouse. In general:
	Joint Tenants hold with rights of survivorship. Their shares pass to the surviving owner.
	Tenants-in-Common hold as separate owners. Their shares pass through their estate plan.
Special	

Nathan Bissonette

Torrens Note — If the relief sought is to the tenancy shown on a Certificate of Title (example, change tenants-in-common to joint tenants), the case must be brought as a Proceeding Subsequent.

Citations

Minnesota does not have "tenancy by the entirety," only the two tenancies listed above. Minn. Stat. 500.19, Subd. 1.

The presumption is against joint tenancy. If a joint tenancy is not explicitly created, the default setting is Tenants-in-Common. Minn. Stat. 500.19, Subd. 2.

Juridical entities such as corporations cannot hold title in joint tenancy because a juridical entity can never die.

> Blackstone's commentaries, published in 1753:
> This right of survivorship is called by our ancient authors . . . the *jus accrescendi,* because the right upon the death of one joint-tenant accumulates and increases to the survivors . . . . And this *jus accrescendi* ought to be mutual; which I apprehend to be one reason why neither the king, **nor any corporation**, can be a joint-tenant with a private person. For here is no mutuality: the private person has not even the remotest chance of being seised of the entirety by benefit of survivorship; for the king and the corporation can never die.

Patton on Titles, Chapter 8, Section 408, page 311 (volume 2)
> A corporation can hold by tenancy in common, but not as joint tenants, since survivorship rights would not apply.

Real Estate Reference Guide for Judges

Title Standard 20 – "Natural persons" only
The title standard initially was written in 1946. Under the common law existing in 1946, corporations could not be joint tenants so using the words "natural persons" in the title standard was a correct statement of the law. None of the amendments to Minn. Stat. 500.19 reversed the prior common law. Title Standard 20 remains a correct statement of the law. Only natural persons can form joint tenancies.

The rebuttable presumption is that all co-owners hold equal shares, unless otherwise stated.
Lendzyk v. Wrazidlo, A14-1331, unpublished (Minn. App. 2015)

Tenancy does not over-ride **marital rights**. Whether spouses own as Joint Tenants or as Tenants-in-Common, both must join in conveyances. See "Marital Rights" above.

Tenancy does not over-ride **spousal rights** in Probate. The surviving spouse has special rights to the homestead and to the value of non-probate transfers such as Joint Tenancies, in addition to rights in land held as Tenants-in-Common which passes through the probate estate. A detailed analysis of **spousal rights** in Probate is beyond the scope of this summary sheet. We recommend you call the Probate Office for more complete answers to specific questions.

Rule 215 Minn. Gen. R. Prac. requires an order in civil case that affects Torrens land to be approved as to form by Examiner of Titles before presentation to court.

2019 update:
Severance of Joint Tenancy

Nathan Bissonette

Joint tenancy may be converted into tenants-in-common by recording an instrument that severs the joint tenancy. A court may order severance. Bankruptcy and divorce also sever a joint tenancy. Minn. Stat. 500.19, Subd 5.

A third party has no power to sever a joint tenancy between married persons, for example, to sell the house to enforce a federal tax lien owed by only one spouse.
O'Hagen v. United States, 86 F.3rd 776 (8th Cir. 1995)
Kipp v. Sweno 683 N.W.2d 259 (Minn. 2003).

There is an on-going debate whether the actions of one joint tenant severs a joint tenancy between the other joint tenants. For example, Tom, Dick and Harry own property as joint tenants. Harry conveys his interest to Jane. Harry's conveyance effects a severance of Jane's portion – she becomes tenant-in-common with Tom and Dick, everyone agrees on that.

But as between Tom and Dick, are they still joint tenants with each other, or has their joint tenancy also been severed?

Commentators saying "No, Tom and Dick's joint tenancy has not been severed," include:
Sathoff v. Sutterer, 869 N.E.2d, 354 (Ill. Ct. App. 2007). Illinois case, informative but not binding.

"Patton and Palomar on Land Titles," Third Edition, Section 223, page 533, citing *Cortelyou v. Dinger*, 62 Misc.2d 1007, 310 N.Y.S.2d 764 (1970). New York case.

"Principles of Property Law," Samantha J. Hepburn, page 429, citing *Wright v. Gibbons*, 78 CLR 313, (1949). This is a commentary on Australian law which is informative (because American common law devolved from the same source), not binding.

> "Yet, if one of three joint-tenants aliens his share, the two remaining tenants still hold their parts by joint-tenancy and survivorship: and, if one of three joint-tenants releases his share to one of his companions, though the joint-tenancy is destroyed with regard to that part, yet the two remaining parts are still held in jointure . . .."
>
> > "Commentaries on the Laws of England" (1765-1769), Sir William Blackstone, Book 2, Chapter 12, Of Estates in Joint-Tenancy.

There does not appear to be Minnesota law directly on point, so the issue must be considered an open question. If anyone finds a definitive answer, the Office of the Ramsey County Examiner of Titles would be grateful to learn of it.

2021 update:
Termination of joint tenancy

> Joint tenants enjoy rights in the entire parcel. When one joint tenant dies, her joint tenancy interest is not transferred to the others, her joint tenancy interest simply disappears. For that reason, a lien on the deceased joint tenant's interest does not become a lien on the surviving joint tenants' interests.
> *Application of Gau*, 41 N.W. 2d 444 (Minn. 1950) (also cited as *Gau v. Hyland*).

> Author's note: This is an important and little-understood distinction:
> - A deed from a living person is effective upon delivery (subject to the race-notice recording rules). A lien or encumbrance upon the owner's interest passes to the buyer.
> - Title held as sole owner or tenant in common passes at the moment of the owner's death, subject to administration by the court. Recording the PR's Deed, Order of Distribution or Decree of Distribution merely

provides documentation of the transfer which already occurred. If there was a lien against the deceased person's interest, it passes with the land to the heirs/devisees.

- The joint tenancy interest does not transfer, **it disappears.** The surviving joint tenant already owned the entire property, she/he acquires no additional rights when the first-to-die joint tenant passes. Recording the Affidavit of Survivorship does not transfer the joint tenancy interest, it merely provides documentation of the disappearance of that interest. A lien or encumbrance upon the joint tenant's interest does not pass to the surviving joint tenants, the lien disappears, as well.

2022 update:
Sisters Jane and Lynn sought to refinance their lake property. Their parents co-signed the loan. To provide the parents with an interest in the property, Jane and Lynn gave a deed to themselves and their parents as tenants in common. The granting clause of the deed did not specify percentages of ownership but a handwritten note on the second page said "1%." The Registrar of Titles issued a Torrens Certificate of Title showing the parents as 50% owners. Remanded for findings on the parties' intent, whether the parents were 'good faith purchasers' and whether the result under Torrens law 'violates notions of justice and good faith" citing *In re Collier*, 726 N.W.2d 799 (Minn. 2007). The Court of Appeals also noted prior cases holding that revising a Certificate of Title based on oral testimony which contradicted the written deeds and handwritten notes was acceptable, and that a certificate of title can be amended based on a claim of equitable relief.

In Re Serrano, unpublished, A21-0164 (Minn. App. 2021)

2023 update:
This 1919 case was found while researching another matter. It is included because it contains a helpful explanation of the court's

reasoning. Where two persons are named grantees in a deed, the presumption is that their interests in the land conveyed are equal. This presumption is not conclusive and the true interest of each may be shown. The fact that Grantees are married does not change the rule.

Dorsey v. Dorsey, 142 Minn. 279, 171 N.W. 933 (Minn. 1919)

Transfer on Death Deed

Summary	Not a separate cause of action; probate avoidance tool.
Statute	Minn. Stat. 507.071
Limitations	None
Necessary Parties	Persons whose interests would be affected by the change, typically other owners and heirs who would be divested or dis-inherited by the change.
Elements Burden of Proof Standard of Proof Defenses	)) TODD disputes heard in Probate Ct.))
Oddities	One TODD may cover multiple parcels. Must be properly recorded in a county where at least some of the land is located, before the Grantor-Owner's death.
Special Torrens Note	"Properly recorded" for Torrens land, means "recorded on the Certificate of Title." Do not bring as a Proceeding Subsequent; litigate in Probate Court. Rule 215 Minn. Gen. R. Prac., requires an order in civil case that affects Torrens land to be approved as to form by Examiner of Titles before presentation to court.

Real Estate Reference Guide for Judges

Citations
> Conveyance by TODD of homestead subject to judgment was not a fraudulent transfer under Minn. Stat. 513.41-51. Beneficiary took title free of judgment lien.
>> *Kesanen v. Strope-Robinson,* A18-1060, unpublished (Minn. App. 2019)

2019 Update: This section was new in 2019.

2020 Update:
> The "no sale" clause in a contract-for-deed violated when the contract-for-deed buyer recorded a TODD and then died.
>> *Woodard v. Krumrie,* unpublished, A19-0800, (Minn. App. 2020, review denied).

> **NOTE**: The Supreme Court denied review despite the urging of the Real Property Section of the MSBA to hear the matter and to allow the Section to submit an amicus brief arguing for reversal on the grounds the Court of Appeals misunderstood the statute. The holding in this case is controversial and should be applied narrowly.

2023 update:
> The "no sale" clause in a contract-for-deed was not violated when the contract-for-deed buyer died without a will and his interest in the property passed to his heirs by operation of law. The Seller was not allowed to cancel the contract.
>> *Kuhn v. Dunn,* unpublished A22-1298 (Minn. App. 2023)

> **NOTE**: The Kuhn court distinguished Woodard because executing a TODD is an affirmative act which conveys an equitable interest to the Grantee Beneficiaries (an assumption found nowhere in the statute), whereas dying without a Will is a failure to act which conveys nothing. The court did not speculate whether making a Will would also be an

affirmative act which would violate the "no sale" clause. The holding in this case is controversial and should be applied narrowly.

Lender lent Borrower money in exchange for a promissory note (apparently not secured by a mortgage). Lender brought suit against Borrower for default, which Borrower contested. Four months later, while the action was pending, Borrower executed a TODD leaving his property to his daughters, then died. Lender sought to void the TODD as a fraudulent transfer under Minn. Stat. 513.41. Held: the district court erred in dismissing the fraudulent transfer claim.
 Minnwest Bank v. Kalass, unpublished, A22-0502 (Minn. App. 2022)

NOTE: Once again, the Court of Appeals confuses a Transfer on Death Deed with a conveyance. It is not. A TODD simply changes who receives the property after death (from heirs, under intestacy, to grantee beneficiaries, under the TODD), same as writing a Will. The holding in this case is controversial and should be applied narrowly.

Trespass

Summary	A physical invasion onto land without permission or legal right (example, garage built over the lot line).
Statute	Usually pled as declaratory judgment, Chapter 555 or Action to Determine Adverse Claims under Chapter 559, sometimes Minn. Stat. 561.01.
Limitations	Six years, Minn. Stat. 541.05, Subd 1(3); but for a continuing trespass, each day starts a new limitations period.
Necessary Parties	Trespasser; persons with right of possession.
Elements	Trespasser entered lands on which plaintiff had right of possession, without permission or legal right
Burden of Proof	Plaintiff must prove ownership/right of exclusive possession and location of boundary crossed by Trespasser
Standard of Proof	Preponderance
Defenses	Entry did not occur; entry was permissive; entry did no damage.
Oddities	**Order should include** Findings of Fact on ownership, possession, legal description, specific acts constituting trespass, identity of trespasser and amount of damages.

Treble damages for cutting trees is statutory claim under Minn. Stat. 548.05, based on theory trees are personal property, independent cause of action from intentional tort of trespass to real estate. It is often pled with common-law trespass but has separate elements and damages.

Special Torrens Note
If the relief sought is money damages and not an alteration to a Certificate of Title, the case need not be brought as a Proceeding Subsequent, even if the land is Torrens.

Rule 215 Minn. Gen. R. Prac., which requires an order in civil case that affects Torrens land to be approved as to form by Examiner of Titles before presentation to court, does **not** apply to these actions.

Citations
A trespass is committed where a plaintiff has the right of possession to the land at issue and there is a wrongful and unlawful entry upon such possession by defendant.
All American Foods, Inc. v. County of Aitkin, 266 N.W.2d 704 (Minn. 1978)

In the absence of actual damages, the trespasser is liable for nominal damages.
Romans v. Nadler, 14 N.W.2d 482 (Minn. 1944)

Trespass is an intentional tort. Reasonableness on the part of the defendant is not a defense to trespass liability.
H. Christiansen & Sons, Inc. v. City of Duluth, 31 N.W.2d 270 (Minn. 1948)

Real Estate Reference Guide for Judges

Invasion by offensive odors are nuisances, but not trespass.
> *Fagerlie v. City of Willmar,* 435 N.W.2d 641 (Minn. App. 1989)

Invasion by particulate matter (crop dusting) is not a trespass.
> *Johnson v. Paynesville Farmer's Union Cooperative Oil Company,* 817 N.W.2d 693 (Minn. 2012)

Stray voltage is not a trespass.
> *Poppler v. Wright Hennepin Cooperative Electric Association,* 834 N.W.2d 527 (Minn. App. 2013)

Where a building encroached and the court declined to order it torn down, the court conveyed title to the land where the building stood to the encroacher and awarded damages for the value of fee title conveyed plus damages for diminution-in-value of the remaining land, to the landowner who lost title.
> *Minnwest Bank v. RTB, LLC,* 873 N.W.2d 135 (Minn. App. 2015)

Diversion of water is not necessarily a trespass. The upstream owner has the right to cast his waters upon the property of another so long as doing so does not create an unreasonable burden. Crop loss resulting from an obstructed tile line entitles the victim to damages.
> *Matter v. Nelson,* 478 N.W.2d 211 (Minn. App. 1991)
> *Kral v. Boesch,* 557 N.W.2d 597 (Minn. 1996)

For a continuing trespass, the six-year statute of limitations does not run from the initial trespass, so it does not bar the action (*Hebert v. City of Fifty Lakes,* A06-215, unpublished, (Minn. App. 2007), but damages are limited to the six-year period preceding the filing of the action (*Hebert v. City of Fifty Lakes*, 744 N.W.2d 226 (Minn. 2008)).

2018 update:
Pulling and shaking weeds that may have been contaminated with asbestos from a home renovation was not sufficient evidence to show an "unlawful entry" for purposes of asserting a trespass claim.
Moore v. Fletcher, unpublished, A16-1922 (Minn. App. 2017)

www.ingramcontent.com/pod-product-compliance
Lightning Source LLC
Chambersburg PA
CBHW071421180526
45170CB00001B/173